The
BOOK
of WORDS
ספר של דברים

The
BOOK
of WORDS

ספר של דברים

(Sefer shel Devarim)

Talking Spiritual Life,
Living Spiritual Talk

LAWRENCE KUSHNER

Jewish Lights Publishing
Woodstock, Vermont

The Book of Words [ספר של דברים]
Talking Spiritual Life, Living Spiritual Talk
1998 First Quality Paperback Edition

Library of Congress Cataloging-in-Publication Data
Kushner, Lawrence, 1943–
The book of words = [Sefer shel devarim] : talking spiritual life,
living spiritual talk / Lawrence Kushner
p.   cm.
Includes bibliographical references.
ISBN 1-58023-020-2 (Quality Paperback)
ISBN 1-879045-35-4 (Hardcover)
1. Spiritual life—Judaism. 2. Jewish way of life. 3. Judaism—
Terminology. 4. Judaism—Quotations, maxims, etc. 5. Self-
actualization (Psychology)—Religious aspects—Judaism. I. Title.
II. Title: Sefer shel devarim.
BM723.K8672   1993
296.7—dc20   93–29004
                      CIP

10 9 8 7 6 5 4 3 2 1

Manufactured in the United States of America

Book and cover designed and illustrated by the author.

Published by Jewish Lights Publishing
A Division of LongHill Partners, Inc.
Sunset Farm Offices, Route 4
P.O. Box 237
Woodstock, Vermont 05091
Tel (802) 457-4000   Fax (802) 457-4004
www.jewishlights.com

ACKNOWLEDGMENTS

I want to thank Stuart Matlins, Publisher of Jewish Lights, for initially suggesting that I write this sequel to *The Book of Letters* as a primer on spirituality for the 90's. More of his example than he realizes has infused the following pages. His vision and energy is a treasure of the Jewish people. I also want to express my gratitude to Rachel Kahn, the Art Director of Jewish Lights for her keen eye and creative flexibility and to Marie Cantlon, my editor these past many years, for her continued support, wisdom, and sense of humor. Finally I want my wife, Karen, to know that she is still for me a "fountain of gardens, a well of living waters."

LSK
Sudbury, Massachusetts
30 July 1993
12 Av 5753
Erev Shabbat Nahamu

for

Michael B. Rukin

חבר

DEAR FRIEND

(Kha•vaer')

TABLE of CONTENTS

INTRODUCTION

According to the Hebrew Bible, God made the world with words. God just spoke and the world became reality. (The Aramaic for "I create as I speak" is *avara k'davara*, or, in magician's language, *abracadabra*.) Not only are words the instrument of creation, in Judaism they are primary reality itself.

We ordinarily think of words as signifiers—a few syllables which denote something really real. But in Hebrew the word for *word*, *davar*, also means "thing." The word does not need to be made real, it already is. It needs only to be read, spoken, and interpreted. To know the word therefore is to know reality itself.

This, of course, does not protect words from the numbing effects of overuse in any religious tradition. Spoken too often, even the holiest reality begins to sound hollow and loses its ability to create anew. Indeed, some of our most sacred words have come to feel like sawdust in our mouths, no longer able to instruct, inspire, chasten, or nurture. We need to dust them off, shake away the accretions, and wonder again about what they originally might have meant.

The following chapters offer my occasionally unconventional "definitions" of thirty classical Hebrew words, words that describe the spiritual dimension of life, whatever one's faith. Taken together they describe much of Judaism's spiritual spectrum. The definitions do not pretend to be complete, or even lexicographically accurate. Instead, they hopefully offer a way back to the spiritual reality of the words themselves.

Each chapter of *The Book of Words* begins with a Hebrew word and my own English translation. At the bottom of the same page, in smaller type, is a transliteration of the Hebrew along with its more customary English rendering. The transliteration scheme is my best attempt to help the non-Hebrew reader to accurately pronounce each word. In addition to my own definition–essay, each chapter also includes both a biblical citation to anchor the word and a passage from a more recent text indicating the word's growth. Finally, the chapter concludes with a *kavanah*, or personal, meditative exercise designed to enable the reader to "live in the word." Bibliographical sources are listed by phrase and page in a separate section at the end of the book.

AMNESIA

דביקות

The whole world is full of God. (Isaiah 6:3)

But you that cleave unto the Lord your God are alive every one of you this day. (Deuteronomy 4:4)

Being at One with the Holy One of Being is not about becoming the same as God, but about forgetting the boundaries of self. You now realize who you have been all along. You forget, at least for a moment, the mind game of where you end and Creation begins. You understand that you are an expression of Creation: it is in you and you are everywhere in it.

There are many ways we reach for the Holy One (ness). We can attain self-transcendence through our mind in study, through our heart in prayer, or with our hands in sacred deed. We say, in effect, that through becoming God's agent, through voluntarily setting God's will above our own, we literally lose

(d'vey•koot') Unio Mystica

15

our selves and become One with the One whom we serve. It rarely lasts for more than a moment.

The primary obstacle to becoming one is self–awareness, self–consciousness, talking to oneself. And for this reason, high awareness involves stop–ping, ignoring, forgetting the conversation we rou–tinely carry on inside our heads between different parts of our personalities. Such amnesia is another word for self–unification.

When the one who asks and the one who hears are the same, we are who we are. We realize, to our embarrassment, that we have been ourselves all along and only linguistic convention tricked us into thinking that we were someone else. In thinking, praying, and doing what God wants, we become one with God and the Universe. The outer person is an illusion, a figment of language. Only an un–self–awareness remains.

MICHEL OF ZLOCZOV

They would be attached to Him with cleaving, desire and wish. And they would consider themselves to be nothing, understanding that truly without the power of the Creator, blessed be God's Name, who created them and who keeps them in existence, they are nothing just as before the creation; consequently there is nothing in the world but the Creator, the Holy One of Blessing.

Living Spiritual Talk
K A V A N A H

Since the primary obstacle to self–transcendence is an involuntary attitude or mind set, some trick or method of outwitting your normal way of thinking will be necessary.

Do anything with such intensity that you do not realize, until you are finished, that it was you who was doing it. But, of course, this suggestion itself only creates a mental obstacle to its stated goal. For this reason, disregard all advice. "Try" to do nothing. Whenever you can, "be" a servant of the Nameless One. And if all this fails, then perform some religious act, over and over again, until it becomes almost a mime. In this way, even habituation can be pressed into the service of holiness.

AWAKENING

Blessings give reverent and routine voice to our conviction that life is good, one blessing after another. Even, and especially, when life is cold and dark. Indeed to offer blessings at such times may be our only deliverance.

We have specific and unique phrases by which we bless a sacred book before we read it, our children at the Sabbath table, our hands while washing them, the bread we eat, the moon, the fact that we are not slaves, and that the rooster can distinguish between night and day.

"I call heaven and earth to witness against you this day: I have put before you life and death, blessing and curse. Choose life that you and your offspring should live by loving the Lord your God, heeding God's commands and holding fast to God." (Deuteronomy 30:19)

(b'räh•khäh') Blessing

19

We bless dwarfs and trees in first blossom. We bless the hearing of good news and any kind of wine. We bless everything. Or, to be technically correct, we bless the Holy One who stands behind and within them all.

Blessings keep our awareness of life's holy potential ever present. They awaken us to our own lives. Every blessing says, "I am grateful to be a creature and to remind myself and God that life is good."

With each blessing uttered we extend the boundaries of the sacred and ritualize our love of life. One hundred times a day. Everywhere we turn, everything we touch, everyone we see. The blessing can be whispered. No one even needs to hear. No one but the Holy One. "Holy One of Blessing, your Presence fills the universe. Your Presence fills me."

DAILY PRAYER BOOK

The proper blessing to be recited upon hearing bad news: Holy One of Blessing, Your Presence fills creation, You are indeed the judge.

TALMUD

Rabbi Meir used to say that a person is bound to recite one hundred b l e s s i n g s daily…[And on Sabbaths and festivals when the number of blessings in the liturgy is diminished] Rabbi Hiya the son of Rabbi Awia would supplement this number by smelling spices and eating delicacies [which each required the recitation of their own separate blessings.

ספר של דברים

Living Spiritual Talk
K A V A N A H

Every blessing includes the phrase, "Holy One of Blessing, Your Presence fills Creation..." This is the primary rubric of all Jewish prayer. The liturgy is nothing more than a sequence of blessings. There are blessings for enjoyment, fulfilling commandments, daily liturgy, and hearing, seeing and tasting things. Many are listed at the back of any personal prayer book. But no matter how many blessings you "know," there are always new ones, or new conditions for reciting old ones, or even occasions for composing ones never uttered before. Let each day hear a new blessing.

BEING

שבת

I magine a day–long spiritual fiction suspending ordinary time. There would be neither past nor future. Our worldwork would be finished. By closing the books on the past week and refusing to think about the next one, we have nothing left to do. For this reason, on the seventh day there is only the present, simply being alive.

On this day everything we do, and the reasons *for* everything we do, can be only here and now. If our worldwork is done, we

The heaven and the earth were finished, and all their array. On the seventh day God finished the work that God had been doing, and God ceased on the seventh day from all the work that God had done. And God blessed the seventh day and declared it holy. (Genesis 2:1-3)

(shä•bäht') The Sabbath Day

cannot do anything about making it better later. Indeed, *there is no later.*

We quit planning, preparing, investing, conniving, evaluating, fixing, manipulating, arranging, making, and all the other things we do every day. All these things began in the past and will end in the future. We do them, not for their own sake, in the present moment, but with an ulterior motive, for the sake of some later time.

We are obsessed with work. Six days each week we rest so we can go back to work. We play so that we can go back to work. We love so that we can go back to work. One ulterior motive after another. Worrying over the past, living in the future. We are either tied to the past through our uncompleted tasks or compulsively drawn to them through our need for completion in the future. But one day each week there is a day devoted to being present, the seventh day. On that day, we do not have to go anywhere or do anything. Everything is done and we are already here.

ABRAHAM JOSHUA HESCHEL

Technical civilization is [our] conquest of space. It is a triumph frequently achieved by sacrificing an essential ingredient of existence, namely, time. In technical civilization, we expend time to gain space. To enhance our power in the world of space is our main objective. Yet to have more does not mean to be more. The power we attain in the world of space terminates abruptly at the borderline of time. But time is the heart of existence.

Living Spiritual Talk
K A V A N A H

Before leaving for a vacation people usually are consumed with myriad minor tasks, all the little accumulated chores that now clutter the desktop. Unpaid bills, unreturned phone calls, letters to be answered, minor household repairs, things that were not a priority, and kept being postponed but never went away.

Each uncompleted task has its own claim on our freedom. And finishing them liberates us to begin our vacation. Indeed, finishing the last one may actually commence the vacation whether or not we ever leave home. The function of a vacation ultimately may be simply to get us to "clear off our desk."

Now obviously no one can ever complete all the little tasks. Sooner or later, as the vacation departure clock ticks down, we decree arbitrarily that whether or not they are done, we are done. We take whatever remains, stack it all in a neat pile on the corner of the desk, and renounce its claim on us. To do so requires great spiritual self-control.

Well, it is like that with the Day of Being too. Every seventh day we just clear off our desks. Of course we're not finished. And from the looks of our world, hopefully God isn't finished either.

BREATHING

And lo, the Lord passed by. There was a great and mighty wind; splitting mountains and shattering rocks by the power of the Lord; but the Lord was not in the wind.

The letters of the Name of God in Hebrew are *yod, hay, vav*, and *hay*. They are frequently mispronounced *Yahveh*. But in truth they are unutterable. Not because of the holiness they evoke, but because they are all vowels and you cannot pronounce all the vowels at once without risking respiratory injury.

After the wind, an earthquake; but the Lord was not in the earthquake. After the earthquake, fire; but the Lord was not in the fire. And after the fire, the soft barely audible sound of almost breathing. (I Kings 19:11-12)

(hä•shem') The Name of God

27

Moses said to God, "When I come to the Israelites and say to them, 'The God of your parents has sent me to you,' and they ask me, 'What is God's name?' What shall I say to them?" And God said to Moses, "Ehyeh-asher-ehyeh." (Exodus 3:13-14)

God spoke to Moses and said to him, "I am the Lord. I appeared to Abraham, Isaac, and Jacob as El Shaddai, but I did not make myself known to them by my Name Yod Hay Vav Hay." (Exodus 6:2)

This word is the sound of breathing. The holiest Name in the world, the Name of the Creator, is the sound of your own breathing.

That these letters are unpronounceable is no accident. Just as it is no accident that they are also the root letters of the Hebrew verb "to be." Scholars have suggested that a reasonable translation of the four-letter Name of God might be: *The One Who Brings Into Being All That Is.* So God's Name is the Name of Being itself. And, since God is holy, then so is all creation.

At the burning bush Moses asks God for God's Name, but God only replies with *Ehyeh-asher-ehyeh*, often incorrectly rendered by the static English, "I am who I am." But in truth the Hebrew future is unequivocal: "*I will be who I will be.*" Here is a Name (and a God) who is neither completed nor finished. This God is literally *not yet.*

ספר של דברים

MISHNA

On the Day of Atonement, in the Temple in Jerusalem, the High Priest would say, "I pray, O God, your people, the House of Israel, have done wrong, they have transgressed, they have sinned before you. I pray, by Your Name, pardon, I pray, the iniquities, the transgressions, and the sins which Your people the House of Israel, have wrongly committed, and which they have transgressed, and which they have sinned before You, as it is written in the Torah of Moses, Your servant, 'For on this day shall atonement be made for you to cleanse you from all your sins, before God shall you be clean.' And the priests and the people who were standing in the forecourt, when they heard the Ineffable Name come forth from the mouth of the High Priest, used to kneel and prostrate themselves and fall down on their faces and say, 'Blessed is God's Name, the glory of God's Universe is for ever and ever.'"

Living Spiritual Talk
K A V A N A H

If God's Name is the Name of Being, then perhaps breathing itself is the sound of the unpronounceable Name. Find a place and a time that are quiet enough to hear the sound of your own breathing. Simply listen to that barely audible noise and intend that with each inhalation and exhalation you sound the Name of Being. It may be no accident that this exercise is universally acknowledged as an easy and effective method for focusing and relaxation.

COMING

תשובה

HOME

T he world endures because of the ever-present yearning and gesture of returning home to our Source. Through this return, all life is reunited with the Holy One of All Being. In the words of the Talmud, "Returning home is the hardest thing in the world, for truly to return home would mean to bring the

When all these things befall you—the blessing and the curse that I have set before you—and you take them to heart amidst the various nations to which the Lord your God has banished you, and you return to the Lord your God, and you and your children heed God's command with all your heart and soul, just as I enjoin upon you this day, then the Lord your God will restore your fortunes and take you back in love. (Deuteronomy 30:1-3)

(*t'shoo•väh'*) Repentance

31

Messiah. Returning home is also the easiest thing to do, for it only has to occur to you to return home and you have already begun."

This going back to our Source is a great longing that flows through and animates all creation. Through apology, repair, and attempting to heal damage done, we effectively rewrite the past. What was once some thoughtless or even wicked act, when set within the present context of meaning, becomes the commencement of a greater healing.

ABRAHAM ISAAC KOOK

Through Returning Home all things are reunited with God. . . . Returning Home is, in essence, an effort to return to one's original status, to the source of life and higher being in their fullness, without limitation and diminution, in their highest spiritual character, as illumined by the simple, radiant divine light. . . . It is only through the great truth of returning to oneself that the person and the people, the world and all the worlds, the whole of existence, will return to their Creator, to be illumined by the light of life. This is the mystical meaning of the light of the Messiah, the manifestation of the soul of the universe, by whose illumination the world will return to the source of its being, and the light of God will be manifest on it.

ספר של דברים

Living Spiritual Talk
<u>K A V A N A H</u>

In the family album or in one of those little frames that stands upright on an end table in your mother's apartment is a photograph of you when you were a child. You have come a long way since those days in many beautiful ways and in a few shameful ones. If you were given a time machine, what would you tell the child in the photo who once was you? Just looking at who you were seems to awaken the possibility that you could go back to that time and, if not relive your life, at least begin again. Just this is the beginning of the return.

D U E S

קרבנות

When you enter the land that the Lord your God is giving you as a heritage, and you possess it and settle in it, you shall take some of every first fruit of the soil, which you harvest from the land that the Lord your God is giving you, put it in a basket and go to the place where the Lord your God will choose to establish God's Name. You shall go to the priest in charge at that time and say to him, "I acknowledge this day before the Lord your God that I have entered the land that the Lord swore to our parents to give us." The priest shall take the basket from your hand and set it down in front of the altar of the Lord your God. (Deuteronomy 26:1-4)

Centuries ago children began their formal religious education with the book of Leviticus. It is difficult to imagine anything more irrelevant. Their first grade text was literally the ancient Temple priesthood manual for slaughtering animals. The pedagogic reasoning seems to have

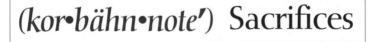

(kor•bähn•note′) Sacrifices

TALMUD

Abraham said, "Sacrifices will suffice while the Temple is standing. But once the Temple is gone, what will become of the people of Israel?" Replied God, "I have already arranged for them passages concerning the sacrifices. Whenever they read about the sacrifices, I shall consider them as having offered sacrifices in My Presence, and I shall forgive them all their sins."

A LEGEND

When Adam and Eve first learned that night would always end with daylight, they offered the first and only unicorn (which had been designated since before the creation of the world for just this purpose) as a sacrifice. And, in so doing, they initiated what has come to be known as organized religion, that is to say, a funny thing you do to help you remember that a greater light precedes and will follow this present darkness.

run that since there can be no contemporary practical benefit, the only possible reason someone would want to learn the laws of sacrifices must be to understand God's words. So therefore let children who are still pure and uncontaminated by the need to use everything study "pure" Divine wisdom for its own sake.

The philosopher Emil Fackenheim, explaining the primal unintelligibility of the biblical sacrificial system, once wryly observed that if we moderns had lived in Jerusalem during the days of the priesthood and wanted to express our gratitude to the Universe, instead of going to a "house of worship" as we now do, we would have gone to the temple, paid a priest to slaughter an animal, and felt like we had accomplished "our business with Heaven."

With the Temple cult's destruction, the ordered ritual of sacrificing animals has been replaced by the ordered ritual sequence of the worship service. When we pray at services, we are only offering sacrifices. Indeed, one could argue that since there are no animal sacrifices to be offered, nor priests to offer them, services are a waste of time. Wasting an animal, wasting time, it's all the same. Perhaps today the most precious thing we have to offer is time. We, who understand that our lives are finite, who cherish every hour of discretionary time, surrender our hours in order to hear and recite a liturgy which has about the same relevance as the laws for slaughtering sacrificial animals. But maybe that's the point.

If you receive something, you must acknowledge the gift, you must give back something precious, be it a statement of gratitude, a reciprocal present, a few hours of your valuable time. Only then may you enjoy what you have received without fearing that it will be withdrawn or that you are a thief.

Living Spiritual Talk
K Λ V A N A H

You have a vegetable garden. In it there is a tomato plant. You have been watching the first green tomato grow. Now it is almost ripe. With something like religious reverence you carefully take this "gift" from the plant and set it to ripen on the window sill above the sink. As soon as it does, you cut it into equal sections for each person at the table and set them prominently atop each salad for the evening meal. What's so special about this first tomato? They're all delicious. Surely even bigger ones will follow. Why not take one of them? The reason is that because within the *first* issue of any species is embodied the regenerative potential for the entire species. All of tomato–ness is in that first fruit. It must be consumed in holiness, returned to the Universe with reverence.

Though it sounds strange, notice how appropriate it also seems to take that same first ripe tomato and simply bury it in the earth next to the plant. The act of reverently and gratefully returning the gift back to its Source accomplishes the same objective. It is the first earned dollar bill taped with yellowing cellophane tape above the cash register at the corner store. What has come first (indeed, that any thing should come at all) does not belong to me. I do not pretend to understand how the universe works. I am only grateful to be alive and receive its nourishment.

גאולה
EXCHANGE

When I was a little boy growing up in Detroit, my mother always shopped at the Big Bear Market (I think that is what it was called) because they gave *S & H Green Stamps*. These were the grocery store precursors of frequent traveler air miles. The stamps came in small perforated and gummed sheets and were *But Moses said to the people, "Have no fear! Stand by, and witness the deliverance which the Lord will work for you today; for the Egyptians whom you see today you will never see again. The Lord will battle for you; you hold your peace." (Exodus 14:13-14)*

awarded in proportion to each dollar spent. It was my job to lick the stamps and paste them into little newsprint booklets about the size of a *TV Guide*. We kept the booklets fat with stamps in a shoe box on the floor of the front hall closet, and when the box was full we would take its contents to the local *S & H Green Stamp* "Redemption" Center where we would

(g'oo•läh') Redemption

exchange this basically worthless stash of stickum for something of more enduring value like a carpet sweeper or an electric toaster.

That is how I came to learn about redemption: the process of cashing in your chips or exchanging something of seemingly little value for its true worth. Stamps for toasters or slaves for free men and free women, it's all the same. But you can't have one until you relinquish the other.

The act of redemption, in other words, is the process of exchanging something for what it is really worth. When a slave becomes a free person, the slave is redeemed.

The story of the crossing of the Red Sea is the paradigm redemption. Slaves passed through the waters into freedom on the other side. The story says literally that they stepped into the midst of the sea on dry ground. But how could this be? Either it was the sea, in which case it could not have been dry ground, or it was dry ground, in which case it could not have been the sea.

Implicit here is the willingness to risk everything for new life. If you jump into the void you could cease to exist, or you might emerge on the other side a new person. Precisely this gamble is at the heart of every redemption.

סֵפֶר שֶׁל דְּבָרִים

MARTIN BUBER

One Hasidic master spoke of "the hours in the lowest depths when our soul hovers over the frail trap door which, at the very next instant, may send us down into destruction, madness, and 'suicide' at our own verdict. Indeed, we are astonished that it has not opened up until now. But suddenly we feel a touch as of a hand. It reaches down to us, it wishes to be grasped—and yet what incredible courage is needed to take the hand, to let it draw us up out of the darkness! This is redemption."

Living Spiritual Talk
K A V A N A H

Certainly, if someone were being held captive for ransom he or she could be redeemed. But suppose this other person were just a friend who was captive to something less tangible, what then? Help him not to be a slave anymore; in Biblical idiom, liberate her from bondage. The slavery can be an addiction, a compulsion, a phobia, or simply behaving in a nasty way. You cannot work for your own redemption, only another's. Only this will give you the courage to take the hand of your own redeemer when it is offered.

41

ישראל
FAMILY

Now then if you will obey Me faithfully and keep My covenant, you shall be My treasured possession among all the peoples. Indeed, all the earth is Mine, but you shall be to Me a kingdom of priests and a holy people.
(Exodus 19:5-6)

Home is where they have to let you in simply because you're you. And family are the people who live there. They are the ones whom you get whether you like them or not. In the last tally, they may be all any of us have. As Adin Steinsaltz is once alleged to have quipped, "The worst thing about being a Jew is that you have to associate with them."

The power of congregational life comes precisely from this involuntariness of association. We look about the room and realize these people are not friends or even acquaintances; we do not agree with

(*yis•räh•ael′*) Israel

them about much; these are simply people we are stuck with. The often cited teaching of the sages that "All Israel are intermingled with one another," probably means something more like "We are all stuck with one another." This generates a kind of love, both more intense and more complicated than the voluntary variety. These members of our community, just like the people in our family, literally make us who we are.

For this reason, the place where you grew up with your "family," where you became who you are, is called "home." Every subsequent home is only a pale replica of your first home. In this way place too becomes sacred.

TALMUD

You made Me unique in the universe when you said (Deuteronomy 6:4), "Hear, O Israel, the Lord our God is the only Lord;" and I shall make you unique by having it said (I Chronicles 17:21), "Who is like Your people Israel, a nation one in the earth."

Living Spiritual Talk
K A V A N A H

You and your brother or sister (barring only children or more complicated family structures) share the same parents. Yet even though your parents are obviously the same people to you and your sibling, give or take a few years, pretty much the same home, same values, social milieu, how remarkable that your relationships with them are profoundly different. The rules of your respective parent–child relationships are poles apart. What you must do to be a good son or daughter is different from what your brother or sister must do. It is like that with religious traditions too. Though we all share a common "parent," the "rules" of how we must be faithful to that relationship vary from one person and one religion to another. Each is true and holy and proper. Indeed for one person to try to be a good child according to the rules of his brother or sister would be a disaster.

FREEDOM

השגחה

Then Joseph said to his brothers, "Come forward to me." And when they came forward, he said, "I am your brother Joseph, he whom you sold into Egypt. Now, do not be distressed or reproach yourselves because you sold me hither; it was to save life that God sent me ahead of you.… So, it was not you who sent me here, but God.…"
(Genesis 45:4-5, 8)

Free will may be an illusion. This is not to say that our actions are mechanistically pre-determined, or that some people are condemned to lead lives of wickedness and others sainthood, or that people are not morally responsible for their decisions. Rather it is to remind ourselves that there may be more involved in what we do and what happens around us than can be explained by ordinary laws of cause and effect. Indeed, sometimes we exercise more "freedom" by simply trying to be who we are and, in so doing, become who we are meant to be.

(hähsh•gäh•khäh') Supervision

47

In moments of heightened awareness, we often are overcome with the sensation that everything is happening according to a plan. We have merely raised ourselves to a level from which we can comprehend part of this bigger picture. We cannot see the whole thing, but for a moment we discern larger pieces and, above all, our intended place within the whole. And, even more surprising, at such times of "rising to our destiny," we actually feel a heightened sense of freedom. We are "free" to be what Heaven has intended us to be or not, but we are not free to be something else.

This is certainly what Joseph discovers at the end of Genesis when he has become ruler of all Egypt and reflects on the "ap-parently" malicious plot where-by he was thrown into a pit and

TALMUD

Everything is in the hands of Heaven except the fear of Heaven.

sold into slavery. He explains to his brothers, "So now it was not you who sent me here but God" (Genesis 45:8). Joseph now realizes that this is the way things were meant to be from the very begin-ning. The brothers (and we) think we are doing one thing, but Heaven has a different plan.

God is like the Unconscious of the universe, only occasionally visible but always at work.

NAHMAN OF BRATSLAV

We are taught that a person has free will. But at the same time, God is the ruler of the universe. This seems to be a paradox. In order to understand it, you must realize that there are two levels of free will in the world. On one level is a person's own free will. When people choose to carry out the divine commandments and to perform good deeds, they participate in the task of cleansing the creation by choosing good and rejecting evil. A person's actions thus have a profound effect on bringing the Creation closer to its perfection. These individual acts of free will on the part of a person constitute the "arousal from below."

The second level of free will is that which is in the hands of God. At every moment God Godself acts to draw the Creation toward perfection. This constitutes the "arousal from above" through which God Godself cleanses the creation, sifting the good from the evil. Yet ultimately these two levels of free will are not separate. They are both aspects of the same thing. The "arousal from below" sets in motion processes in the worlds above. Conversely, the power to cause the "arousal from below" to come about is only in the hands of God Godself. However it is part of our condition in our present life that we are unable to grasp or understand the way in which these two levels of free will are really one. And it is our very inability to understand it that is actually the source of our own free will.

Living Spiritual Talk
K A V A N A H

Go ahead, do something you were not intended to do.

GARBAGE

You must not eat flesh torn by beasts in the field; you shall cast it to the dogs. You must not carry false rumors. (Exodus 22:30-23:1)

Like eating carrion, hearing derogatory information about another person can make you ill. Would you eat garbage off the street? Then why tolerate auditory filth in your ears!

As our sages have warned, there are three who are involved in every act of gossip: the one spoken about, the one who speaks, and the one who hears. But they startle us with their insight that the one who hears is injured the most. Once the information is heard, even if later disproven, you cannot completely cleanse it from your brain. The suspicion persists. Years later, you meet the person, the object of the gossip. You have reviewed all the facts and are thoroughly

You shall not go about as a tale bearer among your people. (Leviticus 19:16)

(l'shohn' hä•räh') Gossip

convinced the rumor was un-true. But still you remember what you heard, you can't seem to get it out of your head. The gossip continues to subvert your relationship.

There are, of course, a few qualifications to the prohibition against gossip such as repeating information already public or protecting others from the unscrupulous.

But how do you know the veracity of something before you hear it? You don't. For this reason, as an act of self-protection, you prohibit information about another human being from entering your ears. You say to the purveyor of gossip, "Please stop. I don't want to hear."

Personal holiness involves what you take into your body, visually, aurally, or orally. You are what you see and hear every bit as much as you are what you eat.

MAIMONIDES

Who is a tale-bearer? Anyone who takes stories and goes around from one person to another saying things like, "So-and-so said this" or "Such-and-such a statement I have heard about so-and-so." Even if what he says or repeats be true, the tale-bearer destroys the world!

It is all the evil tongue whether it be in the victim's presence or in his absence; anyone who says anything which, if repeated, might damage another physically or financially, distress him or upset him, is guilty of evil speech.

Why such a big deal about gossiping? Because words are ultimate reality. God created the world by uttering words. "And God said, 'Let there be...' And there was." Therefore we too can destroy as we speak.

Living Spiritual Talk
K A V A N A H

Our ears are insatiable. Hearing dirt about others gives us a sense of power over them. But in truth, because they know the truth and we will probably never know, it is they who have power over us. Hearing dirt about others also fosters the illusion that we are better than they when, in fact, by eating gossip off the street and contaminating our minds, we are the ones made worse.

We are junkies for gossip. Try to make it for three hours without saying anything about another person. Or, even more difficult, try to make it for three hours without hearing something about someone. Push the words away with your palm and say, "Let's talk about something else."

IMAGERY

עֲבוֹדָה זָרָה

Why all the fuss about idolatry? So what if you're stupid enough to talk to a statue, surely no harm could come from that. Worshipping an idol is not the problem. The danger is allowing yourself to imagine that God could look like anything at all, for such a god is not only motionless but predictable,

You shall have no other gods besides Me. You shall not make for yourself a sculptured image, or any likeness of what is in the heavens above, on the earth below, or in the waters under the earth. You shall not bow down to them or serve them. (Exodus 20:3-5)

The Lord spoke to Moses, "Hurry down, for your people, whom you

brought out of the land of Egypt, have acted basely. They have been quick to turn aside from the way that I enjoined upon them. They have made themselves a molten calf and bowed low to it and sacrificed to it, saying: 'This is your god, O Israel, who brought you out of the land of Egypt!'" (Exodus 31:7-8)

(äh′vo•däh′ zäh•rä′) Idolatry

55

frozen, dead. And so are those who worship such a god. When Ultimate Holiness stands still, you die.

Idolatry is not the worship of carved or molded fetishes in the image of God. It is the dangerous, ubiquitous, and seductive fantasy that God can have any image at all. We want so much, for the most pious reasons, to capture just a spark of the divine so that we can summon it when we are tired or afraid. Just a memento of intimacy imagined.

It is true that everything contains something of the divine. But nothing looks like God, because God doesn't look like anything. There is simply nothing to see.

MIDRASH

The Rabbis say: Seeing that there is no reality in idols, why does Scripture apply the term "deity" to them? Rabbi Phinhas ben Hama said: In order to assign a reward to anyone who turns away from idolatry. God said: Although there is no reality in it, yet as soon as a person turns away from it, I account it to that person as if he or she were worshipping the One who really is and as if that person came to Me.

Living Spiritual Talk
K A V A N A H

Find a snapshot of someone you love, not one that's irreplaceable or valuable, just one that is a reasonable and recent likeness. Look at it for a few minutes. Now tear it up. Destroy it. Certainly not because you wish them harm, but because you want to remind yourself that they are not the photo, they never were. You cannot imagine who they really are. You cannot comprehend, summon, or own them. What you have, even when you see them, is only a crude evocation of who they really are. How much the more so with the Holy One of Being who has no image at all.

INTEGRITY

Surely, this instruction which I enjoin upon you this day is not too baffling for you, nor is it beyond reach. It is not in the heavens that you should say, "Who among us can go up to the heavens and get it for us and impart it to us, that we may observe it?" Neither is it beyond the sea, that you should say, "Who among us can cross to the other side of the sea and get it for us and impart it to us, that we may observe it?" No, the thing is very close to you, in your mouth and in your heart, to do it. (Deuteronomy 30:11-14)

The word *kavanah*, at its root level, simply means "direction" or "aim." Among the pious it connotes "intention," and, specifically, intending that one's act be done in response to a divine request. "I do not do what I am about to do because I want to (even though I might), nor even because it makes sense (even though it may), but

(käh•väh•näh') Sincerity

59

because Heaven desires it." (Indeed we have a whole category of religious acts which are precious precisely because they make no sense, such as the Leviticus 19:19 prohibition against wearing garments made from a mixture of linen and wool. Performing them offers no personal pleasure save the joy of knowing that you are serving the Creator.) Thus we say that any given religious act, whether ritual or ethical, can be done from habit without spiritual intention or it can be done solely "for the sake of Heaven," that is, with *"kavanah."* What you do and what you mean are aligned, are the same.

Finally *kavanah* came to mean something you do or meditate upon as a focusing preparation *before* you begin the actual religious act itself. Thus a *kavanah* is a spiritual gesture designed to unite our innermost intentions with our outermost acts. The twist, of course, is that once we discover that a particular *kavanah* "works," we instinctively do it all the time, eventually elevating it to the level of a divine request, for surely anything that could unify intention with action must be sacred. But alas, given human nature, once this happens, the power of the *kavanah* itself becomes encrusted with its own habituation. For this reason *kavanot* have very short shelf-lives. They are little things we do or think about to snap us out of our reverie, wake us up, and return us to our lives. They are self-inflicted slaps in the face.

ספר של דברים

DOV BAER OF MEZRITCH

When you begin to pray, you become God's garment and God speaks words through your mouth. Becoming aware of this you will be overcome by awe and reverence. God enters you, as in the phrase from Song of Songs 2:9, "This one peers through the lattice."

Living Spiritual Talk
K A V A N A H

For *"kavanah"* there can be no *"kavanah."*

הִתְלַהֲבוּת
LAUGHTER

T here can be joy in silence or with tears, just as there can be laughter in terror or in pain. When people are joyous, they are at their best: they are generous, kind, grateful, and reverent. Happy families are just that; if they don't actually laugh, they smile a lot. They laugh at jokes, the state of the universe, and, above all, they laugh at them-selves. I am not talking here about ridicule or jest, nor laughter from embarrassment or anxiety. It is a joy to be alive.

And you shall take for yourselves on the first day an etrog, a palm branch, a myrtle, and a willow of the brook, and you shall rejoice before the Lord your God. (Leviticus 23:40)

I'm talking about learning how to dis-cern the humor in even our "holiest" undertakings. If by the word "sacred" we mean that we cannot laugh at it, then it is less than sacred. But conversely whatever occasions joyous laughter turns out to be sacred.

(hit•lä•hä•voot') Ecstasy

Rabbi Nahman of Bratslav used to counsel his students that depression was the most clever disguise of the *yetzer hara*, our evil impulse, and that we must fight with every weapon in our power, even simply having friends tell us one joke after another.

Laughter is so important that Jews have institutionalized it into a holiday. Purim does more than celebrate the foiled attempts of anti-Semites everywhere, it makes us laugh at ourselves. The head of the famous Slabotka Yeshiva, on Purim, would dress up like a horse.

It is interesting furthermore that we have made Purim, which celebrates the foiling of our enemies, into a time for laughter by dressing up like them. Zalman Schachter-Shalomi used to say that when the Purim play is over, all the actors get applause, but Haman, the villain, gets the most. Access to the most joyous part of ourselves comes through ritualized reminders that we are as bad as our enemies. On Purim we are enjoined to get so drunk we cannot even tell the difference. Indeed, only our ability to laugh at ourselves keeps us sane and from becoming like them.

I remember how my father used to love to sing "The Red River Valley." He never missed an opportunity to offer a solo. To this day I cannot hear it without crying. Only once did it make me laugh. The organist at the temple in Detroit where he worked played it as a prelude to the funeral. Amazed, people picked their heads up from their tears and one by one, as they recognized the melody, began to smile.

Laughter at sad times does more than relieve tension, it initiates healing. Laughter reminds us of another dimension of our psyche. I suspect that laughter may be able to banish the fiery sword that guards the entrance to the Tree of Life. This may be why the Hasidim were fond of punning that *Yom Kippurim* could also be mistranslated not as the day of Atonement but a day like *Purim*. According to one tradition, after the Messiah comes, observance of all the holidays will be abrogated except the day when we laugh at our enemies and ourselves.

A woman I know had a son who was killed in the Israeli army. She tells of the funeral and a joke she found herself thinking at that terrible time. "Please don't think me escapist or irreverent. But there I was, walking in the cortege to the cemetery, with my brother and other son, right behind the jeep carrying the casket and flanked by six soldiers. I wanted so much to reach out and touch the coffin one last time but the procession was so military, I was afraid. And suddenly I found myself thinking, 'I know parents have to let go of their children, but this is just ridiculous!' And at that moment, she confided, "I realized that I was going to make it."

MAIMONIDES

The simcha *that one makes in the fulfillment of a commandment and in love of God who commanded them is a very high form of prayer. One who restrains himself from such rejoicing deserves to be punished, as it is said, "Because you did not serve the Lord your God with joy, and with a good heart" (Deuteronomy 28:47). And anyone who is arrogant, cares about his own dignity, and honors himself in his own eyes on such occasions, he is both a sinner and a fool. On the contrary, one who humbles himself and makes light of his body on such occasions, achieves greatness and honor, for he serves God out of sheer love.*

Living Spiritual Talk
<u>K A V A N A H</u>

Two peanuts were walking down the street. One was assaulted…peanut.

66

LIFE
מעשה

King David flew into a rage against the man, and said to Nathan, the prophet, "As the Lord lives, the man who did this deserves to die! He shall pay for the lamb four times over, because he did such a thing and showed no pity." And Nathan said to David, "That man is you!" (II Samuel 12:5-7)

Elie Wiesel once suggested that not everything that happened is true, nor did everything that is true necessarily happen.

Sometimes stories can be true without ever having happened. The story of the garden of Eden, for instance, obviously never happened the way it is told. Snakes don't talk, fruit doesn't contain the secret of life, and people don't wear clothing made from fig leaves. But the story is true. In metaphoric language, to be sure, the legend describes a drama that

(mäh•äh•seh') Story

occurs in the lifetime of every human being. We are not guilty because Adam and Eve were; but we are guilty in precisely the same way. The story is true not because it happened, but because it happens generation after generation. That's why we keep reading it.

The stories which describe the events of our lives are true insofar as they resemble the great archetypic myths. The best movies help us imagine the archetype. Movies are box office hits because they manage (like all great art, often despite the conscious designs of their creators) to portray a mythic truth. When a life experience replicates the great story, we often surprise ourselves by saying, "Wow, my life here is so real, it resembles a movie!" And conversely, movies strike us as true beyond their stories when they seem to capture something of the truth that lies beneath the surface of all creation. This is what we mean when we say that scripture is holy: It speaks the truth beneath the surface. Indeed, the literal text is only a mechanism. As the rabbis used to say, the Bible could not merely be the stories it tells, for we could easily tell better stories!

All the great moments of our lives transcend our lives. We cease to be autonomous actors and find ourselves "taken over" by some ancient script. The bride and the groom who marshal all their energies to fashion a creative wedding are, in the last analysis, only Adam and Eve all over again. Indeed, only to the extent that they are able to permit the great myth to guide their actions and words will their wedding be complete. We give ourselves over to the Great Story, allow ourselves to be carried along by its universal truth. We taste eternity.

SEFAS EMES

Rabbi Simcha Bunam of Przysucha used to explain the meaning of Deuteronomy 29:3 "And not until this day has the Lord given you a heart to understand, eyes to see, nor ears to hear." He taught it meant that all the miracles and wonders which the Holy One did for Israel in the wilderness were supernatural. They were only for that particular time and place. But now, as we conclude the end of the story in Deuteronomy, the entire Torah has been completed for them. Indeed the Torah has been made from their very lives, made from this into a fixed institution for the generations.

Living Spiritual Talk
K A V A N A H

Tell a friend of a time when you felt closer to God than usual. Not a psychedelic light show, just an ordinary, everyday garden variety of heightened awareness of a sacred moment. Do it in the third person singular, present tense. Make it a three sentence story. For example, "This guy is waiting at a red light in rush hour traffic when out of the corner of his eye he catches sight of a child petting a dog." All religious revivals, be they individual or communal, share a concomitant resurgence of the narrative art form.

LOVE

אהבה

My beloved has gone down to his garden, to the beds of spices, to browse in the gardens, to pick lilies. I am my beloved and my beloved is mine. (Song of Songs 6:2-3)

How do you love people? You do selfless things for them. You do things which don't necessarily benefit you. Sometimes they don't benefit you in any way at all. In this sense, every favor can be the beginning of love or at least its repair. Each favor is a gift of self that says, "You mean more to me than me. I may not

Jonathan and David made a pact, because Jonathan loved him as himself. Jonathan took off the cloak and tunic he was wearing and gave them to David, together with his sword, bow, and belt. (I Samuel 18:3-4)

(eh'•khäd') One

71

understand your motive; it is enough for me to know that you desire it."

This is also the idea behind religious deeds. We cannot comprehend why God wants what God wants. Indeed, the more incomprehensible, the more likely we do them solely in response to the divine and not for some baser, ulterior, secret, personal motive. Besides, if they made perfect sense, we'd do them ourselves, without being asked.

Dr. David Sperling has observed that Deuteronomy 6:4–5 (traditionally read as a declaration of monotheism) may actually mean "Hear O' Israel, the Lord is your God; love God; love God with all your heart, with all your soul, and with all your might."

This may explain the relationship between loving and being one. When you love someone, you set your self out of the way, and then you can be one with your lover. But, of course, no sooner is your self "out of the way," than you are also one with yourself. No longer any illusion of some interior self set over against an exterior one. Only no self can comprehend and unify all of you. This may be why love is so fulfilling (and comes as such a surprise to so many).

ZOHAR

Torah calls out…every day, in love…a lovely princess, beautiful in every way and hidden deep within her palace. She has one lover…Out of his love for her, this lover passes by her gate constantly…She opens a little window in her hidden palace and reveals her face to her lover, then swiftly withdraws, concealing herself…And he knows that out of love for him she revealed herself for that one moment to awaken love in him.…Once he has grown accustomed to her, she reveals herself face to face and tells him all her hidden secrets, all the hidden ways, since primordial days secreted in her heart.

Living Spiritual Talk
K A V A N A H

When you first fell in love, your lover could do no wrong. All you need do to reawaken that love is remind yourself (and your lover) of your original judgment. "In my eyes you can do no wrong." And after a while your lover begins to feel so secure that he or she will want to do even better.

MONEY

צדקה

In a universe divided between body and spirit, money is the grossest of matter, and, perhaps, even the source of evil itself. But if matter and spirit are of the same order, if the sacred can be found strewn everywhere throughout physical re-ality, then even money can sanctify. For this rea-son, we are measured not so much by what we buy, but by what we give.

"When you reap the harvest of your land, you shall not reap all the way to the corners of your field, or gather the gleanings of your harvest. You shall not pick your vineyard bare, or gather the fallen fruit of your vineyard; you shall leave them for the poor and the stranger." (Leviticus 19:9-10)

The main obstacle to generosity is forgetting where our money came from. I do not mean who wrote the checks, paid your wages, printed the

(ts'däh•käh') Charity

currency, or even how we earned it. I mean by what combination of skill, luck, grace, and blessing from on High have we wound up with this money in our hands. Where did it come from; how did we *really* get it? When asked this way, only one thing is clear: We do not own what we possess. Like land, which belongs to God, we are stewards but never owners. And if we remember that all our possessions are loaned to us on trust, then we can be satisfied with much less.

After all, when do we have enough? Wealth cannot be measured in absolute dollars. It is the highly subjective sensation of having more than enough, so much that there is money to give away. For this reason, wealth is a function of generosity: The more you give, the richer you feel.

TALMUD

In the world to come, the Holy One of Blessing will bring the evil impulse and slay it in the presence of the righteous and the wicked. To the righteous it will appear like a high mountain, to the wicked like a single hair. Both will weep. The righteous will weep and exclaim, "How were we able to subdue such a lofty mountain?" The wicked will weep and exclaim, "How were we unable to subdue a single hair like this?"

Living Spiritual Talk
K A V A N A H

Share the amounts and recipients of your charitable giving with your children. They know how much you spend on your house, your car, your vacation. They know how much you earn. If the thought of their reaction embarrasses you, then perhaps you need to increase your giving so that the sharing of such information will occasion pride and gratitude for how much you can give.

POISON

נְטִירָה

You shall not hate your kinsfolk in your heart, you must tell him when he has hurt you, but do not commit a sin on account of him. You must not take vengeance; you must not bear a grudge against one another. (Leviticus 19:17-18)

According to the Torah and later rabbinic tradition, there is only one way to let go of a grudge. "You must tell someone when they have hurt you." There are even elaborate scripts to follow for the person who has been hurt. You must not tell them in a way that only injures them back, since that would be taking vengeance. For instance, you must not remind them of the injury in public, so as to embarrass them, nor do you give a twist to the knife so as to cause pain, nor do you tell them in such a way that they have no opportunity to respond in a face-saving way.

(n'tee•räh') Grudge

79

MAIMONIDES

Here is an example of what it means to bear a grudge. Reuben says to Simon, "Sell me this house or loan me this ox." Simon refuses. After a while Simon comes to Reuben wanting to borrow something. Reuben says, "Go ahead. Help yourself. Since I am not like you, I won't treat you the way you treated me." Acting in this way violates the commandment against bearing a grudge. You must blot it out of your mind and not bear a grudge, for as long as you bear it in mind you will be in danger of taking vengeance. Therefore, Torah teaches us not to bear a grudge so that we can entirely blot out the wrong from our memory.

Grammatically, grudges are direct objects. They require transitive verbs. You can't just "have" a grudge—you must "bear" a grudge or "carry" one. They are things we deliberately choose to haul around.

In bearing a grudge, we have transformed the hurt from something we once received into something we now carry or guard. Almost as if, in our inability to repay the pain we felt, we tenaciously carry this little vial of grudge–toxin. Not quite willing to do the other person harm, not quite able to spill it out and forget it. "You hurt me so much. But I am a nice person so I won't hurt you back. Instead, in very small doses, I will just poison myself for the rest of my life. I will carry around the injury you caused me as a special part of my psyche. I will watch it and guard it. But I'll never tell you."

80

In this way, each grudge takes on a life of its own. Like a parasite, living in our past, demanding ever increasing amounts of unconscious attention, it feeds on our vitality. With each passing week, month, year, even though we may have lost all but a fleeting awareness of our hurt, the grudge becomes more and more important.

HASIDIC

It was said of the Gaon, Rabbi Shaul Katznelboegen, that because Purah, the angel of forgetfulness, had no power over him, he had the most exceptional memory there ever was: during his lifetime he forgot nothing of whatever he heard or saw. But if someone sinned against him or insulted him, this he forgot at once.

And as the grudge anchors us to something long gone, it denies a part of us from being here in the present. It requires more and more psychic energy. It burrows deep into our personality, sapping our joy and our happiness. Often we do not even know it is there, until we try to feel joy. A grudge can be detected in the extra muscular effort required to produce a smile.

Living Spiritual Talk
K A V A N A II

Take a moment and think of someone you're still mad at. Nothing big, only that you'd get some pleasure if the person got a parking ticket or spilled food on a new suit. If you can think of such a person, you're still bearing a grudge.

POLITICS

Energy in the form of light is trapped in gross matter. Sparks of holiness are imprisoned in the stuff of creation. They yearn to be set free, reunited with their Source through human action. When we return something to its proper place, where it belongs, where it was meant to be; when we use something in a sacred way or for a holy purpose; when we

You shall not wrong a stranger or oppress him, for you were strangers in the land of Egypt. You shall not ill-treat any widow or orphan. If you do mistreat them, I will heed their outcry as soon as they cry out to Me, and My anger shall blaze forth and I will put you to the sword, and your own wives shall become widows and your children orphans. If you lend money to My people, to the poor among you, do not act toward them as a creditor: exact no interest from them. (Exodus 22:20-24)

(t'koon') Repair

No, this is the religious observance I desire: to loosen all the fetters of wickedness, to untie the cords of lawlessness. To let the oppressed go free, to break every yoke. It is to share your bread with the hungry and to take the wretched poor into your home. When you see the naked, clothe him. Do not turn away from people in need. Then shall your light break forth like the dawn. (Isaiah 58:6-8)

treat another human being as a human being, the captive sparks are released and the cosmos is healed. This liberation of light is called the Repair of Creation.

The process occurs also within each individual. According to one legend, once there was a primordial person as big as the whole universe whose soul contained all souls. This macro–anthropos was the highest form of the Creator's self–manifestation. Light beamed through the human's eyes, nose, and mouth.

This person is identical with the universe and, for this reason, each human being is at the same time both riddled with divine sparks and in desperate need of repair. Each person is the whole world. And every human action therefore plays a role in the final restitution. Whatever we do is related to this ultimate task: To return all things to their original place in God. Everything a person does affects the process.

MIDRASH

Rabbi Elazar said, "The whole Torah depends upon justice. Therefore God gave the detailed commandments about justice beginning

*in Exodus 21 immediately after the Ten Utterances, because when
people transgress justice, God exacts retribution from them and
thereby instructs humanity. Sodom was not overthrown until the
people of Sodom neglected justice, and the people of Jerusalem were
not banished until they disregarded justice.*

Living Spiritual Talk
K A V A N A H

In order to be politically effective you need a
sense of where you are in the universe and where
the universe is in you. You must have a realistic
appraisal of your power, that is, where you stand,
and you must have a sense of the spirit of the times.
Both are necessary. What kind of clout can you
muster "over" and "with" others and what is happening in "these" times?

Politics is getting others to join you. You can use
this power to help others who have less to get more.
You may do so through confrontation or coalition,
force or persuasion. If you do nothing, those in
power will certainly use your inaction to increase
their power. The process begins with the morning
paper.

REMEMBERING

And when in time to come your child asks you saying, "What does this mean?" you shall say to him, "It was with a mighty hand that the Lord brought us out from Egypt, from the house of bondage." (Exodus 13:14)

Memory is the connections. Meaning comes from what something is connected to. Something unconnected, unassociated with, unrelated to anything is literally meaningless. Conversely something connected, associated, linked with many things is supercharged with meaning. And the farther back in time the connections go, the greater the meaning. By joining pieces of our lives together we create ourselves, free ourselves. It's all in the order and the sequence. For this reason, memory may be

And you shall tell your child on that day, saying, "It is because of that which the Lord did for me when I came forth from Egypt." (Exodus 13:8)

(say'•der) Order

more in the way things are stored, rather than what is stored.

It is not accidental that the great feast of remembering our redemption, is called simply: The order. The arrangement and interconnectedness of each of the parts preserves the message, the meaning. The story, for instance, ends with redemption, not with slavery, first come the questions, then the answers, because I was once a slave, I must know how it feels.

We take a memory of four hundred years of slavery and set it into a larger context of liberation and redemption. We then celebrate that slavery with a banquet. We further find in those four hundred years of servitude a continuing admonition to be ever mindful of the affliction of others. We find purpose and mission in our slavery. If slaveries can become freedoms and miseries can become meaningful, then the game is never over. And we can offer a new version of Yogi Berra's famous insight into the life game. It's not that "It ain't over till it's over," but rather "Even when it's all over, it ain't over!" Through the dynamic search for meaning, the past remains eternally fluid before our eyes.

Over the entrance to *Yad VaShem*, Israel's memorial to those who perished in the Holocaust, is inscribed into the stone an aphorism ascribed to the Baal Shem Tov: "Exile comes from forgetting. Memory is the source of redemption." Freud also taught that remembering brings freedom from slavery.

DAILY PRAYER BOOK

The sages have ordained that each person should remember six things every day: The Going out from Egypt, The Sabbath Day, Standing at Mount Sinai, The Way our Parents Tried God in the Wilderness, Miriam, To Blot out the Memory of Amalek.

Living Spiritual Talk
K A V A N A H

Remembering is in the order. What comes before and what comes after. The way to remember what you have forgotten is to recall what happened just before, to set it in a larger context. Sights, sounds, and especially aromas can carry with them powerful associations of other times and ancient dreams. Knowing this, we can deliberately condition ourselves by reserving certain sensations for sacred occasions: a "special" cologne for the Sabbath, a piece of music in preparation for a festival, a text reserved for a sacred time. In so doing we transform our lives into a *"seder,"* an order of remembering.

89

RESPONSE

מצוה

Holiness demands a response, an answer. We cannot simply say, "That's nice. Now on to something else." (Indeed if we can, it was not holiness we knew.) An encounter with the Sacred Unity of All Creation places a demand on our behavior. Sometimes the obligation is nothing more than a promise to remain silent in its Presence or to return to this place again. Other times we are driven to make more sustained changes in our actions and to persuade others to join us. We have "heard" something; something has been "laid upon us." We feel personally obligated, commanded. To ignore this summons would violate the wonder of the moment and the covenant it whispers.

Then [Moses] took the record of the covenant and read it aloud to the people. And they said, "All that the Lord has spoken, we will do and we will hear." (Exodus 24:7)

(*mitz•väh'*) Divine Commandment

This commandment is not a burden. To our surprise, our "response to the Holy" is neither constricting nor limiting. Rather, we are liberated from the vagaries of trend and fashion and reminded that we were created and that we were created for a purpose. And precisely that, and nothing else, is the meaning we seek, the meaning of life.

And these words, which I command you today, shall be upon your heart. Teach them over and over again to your children. Recite them when you are at home and when you are away, when you lie down and when you rise up. Bind them as a sign on your hand and as a symbol on your forehead. Write them upon the doorposts of your house and upon your gates. (Deuteronomy 6:5-9)

Often the response of those who have come before us can sensitize us to hearing this commanding voice and help us give coherent shape to our actions. "When someone asks for money, you must not turn him away empty-handed." "If you put garbage in, garbage will come out." "Remember, you too were once a slave." Other times you will need to fashion your own response, one that is unique to your time and situation. But whether ancient or modern, each day you must listen anew to yourself and to the Commanding Voice of Holiness.

ARNOLD JACOB WOLF

I try to walk the road of Judaism. Embedded in that road there are many jewels. One is marked "Sabbath" and one "Civil Rights" and one "Kashruth" and one "Honor Your Parents" and one "Study of Torah" and one "You Shall Be Holy." There are at least 613 of them and they are of different shapes and sizes and weights. Some are light and easy for me to pick up, and I pick them up. Some are too deeply embedded for me, so far at least, though I get a little stronger by trying to extricate the jewels as I walk the street. Some, perhaps, I shall never be able to pick up. I believe that God expects me to keep on walking Judaism Street and to carry away whatever I can of its commandments. I do not believe that God expects me to lift what I cannot, nor may I condemn my fellow Jew who may not be able to pick up even as much as I can.

Living Spiritual Talk
K A V A N A H

No one explicitly told you how to be a parent, Rabbi Eugene Borowitz observed. One day you simply became one. There was this other human being, your child, with whom you had a relationship. Over the months and years, you both discovered how you had to "be" for one another. Some behavior was required by your mutual relationship, and some was forbidden. Such a living covenant is precisely analogous to our relationship with the Holy One. From trying to live within covenant, commandment emerges. The "other" rarely "tells" you, you just discover how you must act to maintain your end of the deal.

Consider what you do in response to God's presence in your life. You may not hear a thundering

93

Hallelujah Chorus of voices but something more subtle. You become aware you are in the Presence. What then? Silence? Song? Blessing? Candles? Charity? Study? Reaching out to another? Just these are the beginning of the "response."

תפילה
SCRIPT

When you enter the land that the Lord your God is giving you as a heritage, and you possess it and settle in it, you shall take some of every first fruit of the soil, which you harvest from the land that the Lord your God is giving you, put it in a basket and go to the place where the Lord your God will choose to establish God's name. You shall go to the priest in charge at that time and say to him, "I acknowledge this day before the Lord our God that I have entered the land that the Lord swore to our parents to assign us." (Deuteronomy 26:1-3)

Prayer only sounds as if you're talking to God. In truth prayer is reciting the words of a script evolved and evolving over the centuries that gives form to the inchoate yearnings of your innermost being. There is nothing new to say in prayer. Surely God has "heard it all before." What you need to do in order to pray is surrender your own expressions of gratitude and petition to the syntax

> ## *(t'fee•läh')* Prayer

95

of tradition. Only one who can allow the annulment of his or her self is capable of being transformed through the words of prayer, the lines of the script. As long as you cling to your discreet selfhood, you will be unable to transcend your self and your prayers will go "unanswered." For this reason the key to unlocking our most important songs is the script recorded in the prayer book.

Of course, like any good actor, occasional *ad libs*, inflationary modifications, and even forgetting one's lines at times are part of the business. Even the sensation of improvisation has a place, as long as you remember that your "new creation" has already been recited by the Heavenly retinue since before the creation of the world. The script, in other words, is present whether or not the "play" is performed in a human prayer hall.

DOV BAER OF MEZRITCH

You need to think of yourself as nothing. Forget yourself entirely. Pray only for the sake of God's Presence. Only then will you come to transcend time and attain the "World of Thought." No contradictions. No distinctions between life and death or sea and dry land. All the same. . . .This can only happen if you forget yourself entirely. But it cannot be the case while you are attached to the tangible reality of this world. Fixated on the distinctions between good and evil and mundane creation. How otherwise could one possibly transcend time and attain ultimate unification. Thus as long as you remain convinced that you are "something," preoccupied with your daily needs, then the Holy One cannot be present, for God is without end, that is, "nothing," no vessel can contain the One. But this is not so when you think of yourself as nothing.

ספר של דברים

Living Spiritual Talk
K A V A N A H

You cannot set out to put yourself out of the way, any more than you can set as your goal the attainment of love or a sense of community. Such gifts are a coincidental side effect of working with others toward a common goal, caring for a partner through difficult times, or praying regularly. In prayer, of course, the trick is to balance the routine with novelty. You need to know the "script" so well that you can recite the words on "auto pilot" but not so well that the words are habitual. You must know them well enough so that you do not really need the prayer book, yet maintain enough "presence," that the words stream forth fresh, as if you have never spoken them before. In this way you remain balanced on the edge. It does not have to be the entire liturgy; even a single prayer, recited each morning, can serve as a proper beginning. In this way you can make a prayer your own that has been recited for centuries.

SECRECY

אמונה

Faith can either be arrogant, constantly flaunting and proving one's spiritual mettle, or it can be humble, confident in one's abilities and one's world. The former conceals anxiety and insecurity, the latter conceals only itself. A sure sign of genuine reverence is secrecy.

Arrogant faith, blind faith, challenges physical laws and can only be satisfied with increasingly difficult tests. "If you really have faith, then you'll do this." Opposed to such spiritual brinkmanship is a quiet, gentle trust that never calls us to pit our

(eh•moo•näh') Faith

99

piety against the natural order. Instead, we hope only to understand our place in the scheme of creation. As Levi Yitzhak of Berditchev said, "God, I do not need to know why I suffer; I pray only to understand that it is for Your sake."

When we are unsure or afraid, such faith is our support. We say, I have been put here for a reason and I have the ability to do the job that Heaven has set before me. I am guaranteed neither health nor happiness, only that I have the power within me to do what needs be done. Only I can do this, no one else. God has put me where God needs me. If I am very fortunate, someday I may understand.

Such faith enables us to understand that which, until a moment ago, seemed only *strewn* before us has instead been *set* before us. It does not block our way, it is our way. We can only trust Heaven's purpose and our own strength. We have been given what we need to do what we have been called upon to accomplish.

SEFAS EMES

We read in Proverbs 23:3, "Then you will walk securely in your way. . .when you lie down, you will not be afraid." One who trusts in the Holy One, believes that the steps of a person are guided by God and that nothing happens by chance! As Rashi explained, in commenting on Deuteronomy 18:13, it means, "Walk with God wholeheartedly; look to God and don't try to figure out the future, rather accept whatever comes wholeheartedly, then you will be with God and you will be God's portion."

Living Spiritual Talk
K A V A N A H

God puts you where God needs you. You are where you are *supposed* to be. The job you are doing may not be any easier on account of this, indeed it may be harder, even more urgent, but now you are centered, focused, clear. So this is where I am supposed to be. I always thought I was supposed to be somewhere else, doing something else, being someone else. But I realize now that I was mistaken. This does not mean that I can't or will not be doing something else. Just right now, I am where God wants me.

SELF
נשמה

You are (like everyone else who is not crazy) a barely coherent hodgepodge of contradictory thoughts, feelings, and deeds. What keeps you "together" is an imaginary center called a "self." The parts may not organize themselves gracefully, but their totality is literally "you." Without a "self" you would literally disintegrate.

We speak about our self as if it were real even though it possesses neither substance nor location. It

And God blew into his nostrils the soul of life. (Genesis 2:7)

is precisely the same way with God. God is the self of the universe. To say, "There is a God," is to say that creation has some inner coherence and integrity that can make sense. For this reason, our innermost self and God are related. In the same way, our

(n'•shäh•mäh') Soul

103

alienation is self–estrangement and estrangement from God.

The old joke about the madman who thought he was God and explained his delusion by observing that whenever he prayed to God he always wound up talking to himself is more than a joke. Our "self" is the "part" of us we share with God and every other human being, just as it may be what remains of our soul.

TALMUD

The phrase, "Bless the Lord, O' my soul," is used five times in the Book of Psalms. To whom did David refer in these verses? He was alluding only to the Holy One of Being and to the soul. Just as the Holy One of Being fills the whole world, so the soul fills the body. Just as the Holy One of Being sees, but is not seen, so the soul sees but is not itself seen. Just as the Holy One of Being feeds the whole world, so the soul feeds the whole body. Just as the Holy One of Being is pure, so the soul is pure. Just as the Holy One of Being abides in the innermost precincts, so the soul abides in the innermost precincts. Let that which has these five qualities come and praise the One who has these five qualities.

ספר של דברים

Living Spiritual Talk
K A V A N A H

Listen to the sound of your own breathing. Gently hold the tips of your fingers on the inside of your wrist until you can feel your own pulse. Become aware of the blinking of your eyes. This life in you is not your creation. Through it you are given permission to become aware of the interconnectedness of all being. Now look at another human being. The breathing, the heartbeat, the blinking. They are in the other also.

TABLE

מזבח

Beyond ordinary meals there are sacred ones. More than consuming food, holy meals reenact the ritual of the ancient Temple in Jerusalem. They

Make for Me an altar of earth and sacrifice on it your burnt offerings and your sacrifices of well-being, your sheep and your oxen; in every place where I cause My name to be mentioned I will come to you and bless you. And if you make for Me an altar of stones, do not build it of hewn stones; for by wielding your tool upon them you have profaned them. (Exodus 20:21-2)

transform the act of eating into sacrifice. The Hasidim of old used to say that your table is your altar. Indeed, both sacrificial fire and eating are merely different forms of oxidation, a process whereby matter is literally transformed into energy.

(miz•bay'•äkh) Altar

Upon the destruction of the Temple, the Pharisees, the early rabbis, took the cult with all its dietary purity and ritual laws and moved it to each person's kitchen table. In this way, everyone became a priest.

You might think of this ritualization of eating practiced down to this day as a kind of Jewish tea ceremony. The table becomes an altar, the meal becomes sacred in many ways: the meal must be consumed in ritual purity; ideally one should bathe and put on clean clothes; the hands are washed whenever bread is eaten; only kosher food may be consumed; the proper blessings over each food must be recited; people must refuse to carry a grudge to the table by forgiving one another; guests must be waited on; words of scripture must be discussed; the meal should be concluded with grace and songs.

Here is a list of some of the occasions on which sacred meals are commanded: Three during the Sabbath; upon the conclusion of the Sabbath; holidays and festivals, for example, *Purim* and Passover; just before the beginning of *Yom Kippur*; the New Moon; conclusion of a tractate of study; for the first born the day before Passover; annually for the members of the Holy Burial Society; the consecration of a new home; and a mourner's meal.

Food consumed with reverence around a table does more than nourish the guests, it transforms the table, creates a bond among all who partake.

MISHNA

Rabbi Simon said, if three have eaten at one table and have not spoken there words of Torah, it is as if they had eaten of sacrifices of the dead, as it is said, "For all their tables are without God and therefore covered with vomit and filth…"

TALMUD

It is written in Ezekiel 41:22, "The altar of wood three cubits high. . . . and he said to me, 'This is the table that is before the Lord.'" Notice how the verse opens with the word "altar" and concludes with "table." Rabbi Yohanan and Rabbi Eleazar both explain that as long as the Temple stood, the altar atoned for Israel, but now a person's table makes the atonement.

Living Spiritual Talk
K A V A N A H

Begin by ritualizing one meal. Let nothing happen to dilute or injure the sanctity with which it is consumed. Let it begin and end with blessing and song. Let all present make a special effort to make the tone of their conversation appropriate to such an occasion.

TERROR
חיים

O Lord, You have been our refuge in every generation. Before the mountains came into being, before You brought forth the earth and the world, from eternity to eternity, You are God. You return people to dust; You decreed, "Return you mortals!" For in Your sight a thousand years are like yesterday when it is past, like a watch in the night. (Psalm 90:1-4)

Only once you're really scared you're going to die does life take on real meaning. A physician's prognosis identifying the actual cause of your probable death makes each day precious. Everything is supercharged with meaning. You no longer take anything for granted. The most

SIMCHA BUNAM OF PRZYSUCHA

Rabbi Simha Bunam as he lay dying took his wife's hand and said, "Why are you crying? My whole life was only that I might learn how to die."

(khä•yeem') Life

111

trivial sensations are gifts: The smell of a child's hair, the sound of a barking dog, the kiss of a lover, the morning coffee. Each becomes precious. If only there were a way to achieve this heightened gratitude for life without the terror.

We treasure life most when we keep the certainty and imminent possibility of our death before us. Not only will we die, but we could die at any moment. This is not a pitch for life insurance; it is just the truth. All we know is that we are alive right now. Beyond that there simply is no guarantee. No promise about anything six years from now, or six months, or six hours, or even six minutes.

This is one of the reasons we have the Day of Atonement. On this day, we are commanded not to eat or drink. We cannot have sex. We don't perfume, anoint, or deodorize ourselves. We wear white. And by the end of the day, looking around the crowded prayer hall, we realize what has been happening. We appear more like corpses than living men and women. This day has been a rehearsal for our own death.

LEGEND

In his youth King David learned that he would die on Shabbat. *So what do you think his favorite ceremony was?* Havdallah *(the ritual that marks the conclusion to the Sabbath). He couldn't get to it quickly enough.*

HASIDIC

You will only sing as loudly in the world to come as you sing on this earth, so decide right here and now how loudly you want to sing in heaven.

FRANZ ROSENZWEIG

There is no cure for death. Not even health. But the healthy man has the strength to walk alive to his grave. The sick man invokes Death, and lets himself be carried on his back, half-dead from fear of him. Health experiences even Death only "at the right time." It is good friends with him, and knows that when the time comes he will remove the rigid mask and take the flickering torch from the hands of his frightened, weary, disappointed brother, Life. He'll enfold the swooning one in his arms and only then, when Life has closed its eloquent lips, he'll open his eternally silent mouth and say: "Do you recognize me? I am your brother."

Living Spiritual Talk
K A V A N A H

The exercise is simple: Remember that you will die. If you haven't done so already, buy a cemetery plot. There are no excuses. Its value will only increase. If you move, you can always sell it. Your survivors will only have to take the money from your estate or their own pockets. From time to time visit the site you have chosen for your own grave.

Write an ethical will. An ethical will is a letter you write to those who survive you. Tell them how you love them (in case you die before you have the chance), about what you tried to teach by the way you lived your life (so whoever delivers your eulogy won't have to guess), and offer counsel to your family and friends (in the event that you didn't make it clear during your lifetime).

VISION

אמת

Reality may be read through an infinity of lenses. Each refraction carries its own unique bias. Children speak of true or false; adults know better. This is not to say that we have given up on truth, only that we now understand how elusive it is. Nor is it to suggest that truth is relative. Indeed we now suspect there is an absolute truth and that

it is mysteriously connected to what some people call "God." God is not truth but standing in God's presence may be. How matters appear to God, that is true.

We choose our truth by the scope of our vision. To see beyond the present

The Lord came down in a cloud; God stood with [Moses] there and proclaimed the name Lord. The Lord passed before him and proclaimed: "The Lord! the Lord! a God compassionate and gracious, slow to anger, abounding in love and truth."
(Exodus 34:5-6)

(eh'•met)   Truth

115

and beyond the end of our allotted days is to understand why we have been created. As our priorities are rearranged, meaning is revealed, truth glistens. To see our place in creation, in other words, is an act of faith. To comprehend our intended task is our only shot at glimpsing what is enduring and absolutely true. Without the long range lens, nothing is false, but nothing is true either. We are adrift.

And what can be told of what we finally see? Only that All Being at its core is One. Everything else may be false. This may be the meaning of Moses' strange death and inability to enter the promised land. Denied entrance, he was given something better: The ability to see it all from a high mountain, a vision of the truth.

A fact is always the same. Once you learn it, you have it forever. But truth is different. Once you understand it, you are forever changed and "the truth" disappears. And because you are now someone else, you must learn it all over again.

MENACHEM MENDL OF KOTZK

Did the scouts whom Moses sent to scout out the Promised Land lie? Did they fabricate words which were not true? Certainly not. They spoke the truth as they saw it? So why does tradition regard this as a sin? Because a person who is not a liar is not automatically a person of truth. The truth is not always as it appears; it gushes from the depths of the heart, from the sources of faith. Truth and faith are locked arm and arm; no person acquires truth easily or with attention to the superficial but only with toil and effort, with wisdom and understanding. And the spies did not strain for the truth of the word of God. They were not wise enough to stand on the secret of God. They stopped with their vision limited and therefore false, against God's assurance, for this is the absolute truth. Just this was their great sin.

Living Spiritual Talk
K Λ V A N A H

Have someone with whom you shared an intimate and important experience write a paragraph describing what "really" happened. After you have done the same, exchange papers. How could the accounts be so different if only the two of you were there? What is the truth of what transpired?

WATER

טהרה

With pure water will I cleanse you, and you shall be clean; from all your impurities will I cleanse you. A new heart will I give you, and a new spirit will I put within you. I will cause you to follow My teachings, and you shall keep My statutes. You shall be My people, and I will be your God. (Ezekiel 36:25 28)

Death is not bad; it is an inescapable part of life. Nevertheless we are surprised by our aversion to physical contact with it. For all our medical sophistication, death seems to defile us. And only water which carries life, or God, who is the source of life, seem able to purify us.

Every death represents a tear in the curtain, just as any life-making fluid which does not make life, such as seminal emissions or menses, must be treated with great caution. The process of birth is itself a transition from the universe–not-yet–

(tä•hä•räh') Purity

alive to the universe–of–life. A woman who has given birth therefore must be protected from her close encounter with *the other side.*

Our problem is not that we have outgrown these archaic borders between defilement and purity, but that we have forgotten where they are. And when a person has no way of knowing whether he or she is in the universe of life and purity or the universe of death and defilement, that person spends a lot of time in unaware contamination, feeling out of sorts. Water is not only the sea from whence we have come, it is also the medium through which we can return to purity and life.

MIDRASH

With regard to the Israelites, where does Scripture command washing the hands? In the verse in Leviticus 11:44, "Sanctify yourselves and be holy." On the basis of this verse Rabban Gamaliel observed the priestly precautions of self-purification when he ate everyday food. He used to say that obedience to the commandment of washing the hands for the sake of holiness was required not only of priests, but of priests, Levites and Israelites. It was required of every one of them.

ספר של דברים

Living Spiritual Talk
<u>K A V A N A H</u>

Try bathing, but not to get clean. Just stand
under or immerse yourself in natural, flowing water. Find what is called "a well of living waters." Let
them flow over you. Tell no one.

THE WAY

All the people witnessed the thunder and lightning, the blare of the shofar and the mountain smoking; and when the people saw it, they fell back and stood at a distance. "You speak to us," they said to Moses, "and we will obey; but let not God speak to us, lest we die." (Exodus 20:15-16)

T he Way is not a book or a scroll. The Way is a perfect description of all Being. And, since it is perfect, The Way is also the same as All Being. The description, in other words, is identical with The Way itself. Because The Way comes from The Source of All Being, trying to understand The Way constitutes the highest

I make this covenant, with its sanctions, not with you alone, but both with those who are standing here with us this day before the Lord our God and with those who are not with us here this day. (Deuteronomy 29:13-14)

(toh•räh') The Law

activity of mind, just as living in accordance with it is the highest expression of right behavior. In the words of the Proverb: "She is a tree of life to those who hold fast to her."

The Way is the master code for all creation, the infra-structure of being, the blueprint for the world, the source of each person's self. So, in an important sense, to learn about The Way is also to learn about yourself. But you must listen with great care and remove all distracting noise.

Any other noise will drown it out. This was the very same whisper Elijah the prophet heard when he stood on the place where Moses stood and heard the thin, barely audible sound of almost breathing.

This quiet sound and the sustained, silent attention that renders it audible and intelligible places demands on human behavior. To ignore these demands is more than abdicating an existential responsibility. It constitutes sin.

GERSHOM SCHOLEM

According to Rabbi Mendel of Rymanov, all that Israel heard was the aleph *with which in the Hebrew text the first Commandment begins, the* aleph *of the word* anokhi, *"I." In Hebrew the consonant* aleph *represents nothing more than the position taken by the larynx when a word begins with a vowel. Thus the* aleph *may be said to denote the source of all articulate sound, and indeed the kabbalists always regarded it as the spiritual root of all other letters, encompassing in its essence the whole alphabet and hence all other elements of human discourse. To hear the* aleph *is to hear next to nothing; it is the preparation for all audible language, but in itself conveys no determinate, specific meaning.*

Living Spiritual Talk
K A V A N A H

While it is certainly true that a *sefer torah*, the hand-written parchment scroll of the *Five Books of Moses*, is perhaps Judaism's most sacred object and is customarily kept in an elaborate ark or curtained closet at the front of the prayer hall, it is also "just a book" and the ark itself is also merely an extension of the synagogue's library. Arrange with the rabbi of the congregation to "take the book out" some afternoon. Take it to another room in the building where you will not be disturbed. You do not even have to "undress" and open the scroll. Just sit with it, together, both of "you," alone in the room. Listen to it and to yourself. Perhaps someday soon you will learn to read and chant it before the congregation.

YEAST

יֵצֶר הָרַע

Of every tree of the garden you are free to eat; but as for the tree of knowledge of good and bad, you must not eat of it; for as soon as you eat of it, you shall die. (Genesis 2:16-17)

Nothing is intrinsically evil. If something were, then God who is the Source of All Being could not be present everywhere in creation. If something were intrinsically evil, it would have to derive its reality from a force independent from God.

Even our ineluctable urge to do evil is not evil, but only misdirected. Indeed without it, as the legend goes, no hen would lay an egg, no house would be built, no one would go to work. There would be no babies. Psychological energy is mischievous. Left to itself, without direction, it would destroy the world. With direction and struggle, the same energy is a powerful force for healing and life. In the words of the sages, "The

(yeh'•tzer hä•räh') The Evil Urge

greater the person, the greater his or her propensity for doing evil."

We call this urge "the yeast in the dough," for like yeast it is ubiquitous, essential, even indispensable. This libidinous fermenting agent has as its principal weapon the art of disguise. No one in human history has ever set out to do something evil. Instead they believed what they were doing was right and proper. Our desire to label things as "good" or "bad," while of great value, is easily distorted. Most of the terrible things human beings do to one another, they do by telling themselves they are actually fighting against some external evil. But in truth more often than not they have only taken the evil into themselves and have become its agents.

MIDRASH

Nahman said in the name of Rabbi Samuel that the verse in Genesis 1:31, "Behold it was very good," refers to the Good Desire; "And behold it was very good," to the Evil Inclination. Can the Evil Inclination be very good? That would be extraordinary! But if it were not for the Evil Inclination, no one would build a house, take a spouse, or beget children, as King Solomon said in Ecclesiastes, "All labor and skillful work, comes from a person's rivalry with his neighbor."

Living Spiritual Talk
K A V A N A H

When your prayers are going especially well is precisely when you will be assailed by the most lascivious, degenerate thought you have had for months. Your first inclination, naturally, will be to push it away. "Have you no decency! Can't you see what I'm trying to do? Come back later." But of course, the harder you push, the stronger it becomes. Better instead realize that this thought is a dimension of yourself that has sensed this moment of holiness and come up from the cellar to be redeemed. So what you must do, instead of pushing the thought away, is accept it as a part of yourself. Find something sacred even in it. Receive it back into your conscious self. Then you will (both) be redeemed.

YOURSELF
מָשִׁיחַ

The Messiah will only come, goes one legend, when things get so bad we cannot live without him or so good we don't need her. Indeed, we often say that at that time all the contradictions, paradoxes, and antinomies will be resolved.

Love and hate, male and female, even good and evil at last will be in perfect balance. "When the Messiah comes," we will understand how they all fit together and even why it seemed so important that they were once in conflict. But

See, days are coming, declares the Lord, when I will fulfill the promise that I made concerning the House of Israel and the House of Judah. In those days and at that time, I will raise up a true branch of David's line, and he shall do what is just and right in the land. In those days Judah shall be delivered and Israel shall dwell secure. (Jeremiah 33:14-16)

(mo•shee'•ähkh) Messiah

131

MISHNA

In the footsteps of the Messiah presumption will increase and respect disappear. The empire will turn to heresy and there will be no moral reproof. The house of assembly will become a brothel, Galilee will be laid waste, and the people of the frontiers will wander from city to city and none will pity them. The wisdom of the scribes will become odious and those who shun sin will be despised; truth will nowhere be found. Boys will shame old men and old men will show deference to boys.

until that time, the syntax written in our brains cannot simultaneously comprehend a thing and its opposite. Because we cannot comprehend everything on one uncontradictory linear plane, we imagine a time when we won't need to. In this way, the notion of a Messiah is a metaphor for the resolution of all contradiction, when paradox will replace linear logic, right brain supersede the left.

According to Talmud, Rabbi Joshua ben Levi asks Elijah, "When will the Messiah come?" Elijah says, "Go and ask him yourself." Ben Levi finds the "son of David" at the gates of Rome and tells Ben Levi that he will "come today." Ben Levi goes back to Elijah and complains that he has been tricked, for surely the Messiah is not coming today. But Elijah only explains that "Today" refers to Psalm 95:7, which reads, "Today, if you will listen to My voice." In other words, the Messiah will come only when we listen to the voice of God.

"Listening to the voice of God" means attaining a rung of awareness on which hearing God's voice is routine. And once that happens all contradictions are dissolved and you yourself are the Messiah. You already have everything you need and you are where you need to be. Lions will lie down with lambs and then they will eat them because that's what lions and lambs do to and for one another. The way things are just now is messianic. The end of days is now and the Messiah is already here.

ZOHAR

The Messiah will not come until the tears of Esau will be exhausted.

Living Spiritual Talk
K A V A N A H

Tradition wisely warns against "forcing the hand of the Messiah." On the other hand, imagining how much better things could be than they are now only guarantees despair.

Sometimes "the best" is the enemy of "the good." If you allow yourself to measure existence against a perfect standard, life will certainly be miserable. Things, by definition, could always be better than they are now. On the other hand, succumbing to the way things are now is to cease dreaming. The balance, perhaps, is to accept the way things are because, like it or not, for better or for worse, that is literally the only way things are. They, of course, can be different, but only later. To worry about "later" is to miss "now." Remember, one of us may be the Messiah. That possibility shouldn't, but nevertheless does, affect how we treat one another.

ספר של דברים

SOURCES

page

11   *"Read, spoken, and interpreted"*–Handelman, Susan A., *The Slayers of Moses: The Emergence of Rabbinic Interpretation in Modern Literary Theory*, Albany: State University of New York Press, 1982, 3-4.

16   *Michel of Zloczov*–"Via Passiva in Early Hasidism," in *Studies in Eastern European Jewish Mysticism*, Joseph Weiss, ed. David Goldstein, Oxford: Oxford University Press, 1985, 88.

20   *Talmud–Menahot* 43b.

24   *Abraham Joshua Heschel*–"The Sabbath: Its Meaning For Modern Man," in *The Earth Is The Lord's and The Sabbath*, New York: Harper & Row, 1962, 3.

29   *Mishna–Yoma* 6.2.

31   *"The hardest thing"*–*Yoma* 86a,b.

32   *Abraham Isaac Kook*–Abraham Isaac Kook: The Lights of Penitence, The Moral Principles, Lights of Holiness, Essays, Letters, and Poems, *trans. Ben Zion Bokser, New York: Paulist Press, 1978, IV, 2; XII, 9; XV, 10.*

36   *Talmud–Megillah* 31b.

36   *A Legend–The Legends of the Jews*, Louis Ginzberg, Philadelphia: The Jewish Publication Society, 1925, vol. I, 89; vol. V, 116, note 108.

41   *Martin Buber*–"The Man of Today and the Jewish Bible," in *Israel & the World: Essays in a Time of Crisis*, New York: Schocken, 1948, 102.

44   *"Stuck with one another"*–*Shevuot* 39a.

44   *Talmud–Berakhot* 6a.

48 *Talmud–Berakhot* 33b.

49 *Nahman of Bratslav*–Restore My Soul, *Meshivat Nefesh*, trans. Abraham Greenbaum, Jerusalem: Breslov Research Institute, 1980, 73–4; 26 (56).

51 *"Injured the most"–Arakin* 15b.

52 *Maimonides–Mishneh Torah, Hilkot Dayot*, 7:2; 7:5.

56 *Midrash–Devarim Rabba* II.18.

61 *Dov Baer of Mezritch–Maggid Devrav L'Yaakov*, ed. Rivka Schatz-Uffenheimer, Jerusalem: Magnes Press, 1976, par. 2.

65 *A woman–I am grateful to Ms. Pat Fischer for sharing this poignant vignette with me.*

65 *Maimonides–Mishneh Torah, Hilkot Lulav* 8.15

66 *"Two peanuts"–Monty Python.*

69 *Sefas Emes*–Yehuda Aryeh Leib of Ger, in *Itturay Torah*, ed. Aaron Greenberg, Tel Aviv: Yavneh, 1976, (Hebrew), vol. VI, 172.

72 *David Sperling*–"The One We Ought to Love," in *Ehad: The Many Meanings of God is One*, ed. Eugene B. Borowitz, New York: Sh'ma, Inc., 1988, 83–85.

72 *Zohar–Zohar: The Book of Enlightenment*, trans. and ed. Daniel Chanan Matt, New York: Paulist Press, 1983, 123–125.

76 *Talmud–Sukka* 52b.

80 *Maimonides–Mishneh Torah, Hilkot Dayot* 7.8.

81 *Hasidic–Op. cit., Itturay Torah*, vol. IV, 113.

84 *Midrash–Shemot Rabba* 30.19.

93 *Arnold Jacob Wolf–The Condition of Jewish Belief: A Symposium Compiled by the Editors of Commentary Magazine*, New York: MacMillan, 1966, 268.

96 *Dov Baer of Mezritch–Op. cit., Maggid Devarav LeYa'akov*, par. 110.

100 *Sefas Emes–Op. cit.*, Yehuda Aryeh Leib of Ger, in *Itturay Torah,* vol. II, 245 (citing *Genesis Rabba* 68.1).

104 *Talmud–Berakhot* 10a.

104 *The Book of Psalms*–Psalms 103:1,2,22; 104:1,35

109 *Mishna–Avot* 3.3.

109 *Talmud–Berakhot* 55a.

111 *Simcha Bunam of Przysucha*–Martin Buber, *Tales of the Hasidim: Tales of the Later Masters,* New York: Schocken, 1948, vol. II, 268.

113 *Franz Rosenzweig–Franz Rosenzweig: His Life and Thought,* ed. and trans. Nahum N. Glatzer, New York: Schocken, 1953, 213

115 *"Scope of our vision"–I am grateful to Marilyn Newman-Aspel for this insight.*

116 *Menachem Mendl of Kotzk–Op. cit., Itturay Torah,* vol. V, 80.

120 *Midrash–Eliyahu Rabba* 72.

124 *Gershom Scholem–On The Kabbalah And Its Symbolism,* "Religious Authority and Mysticism," trans. Ralph Manheim, New York: Schocken, 1965, 30.

128 *Midrash–Bereshit Rabba* 9.7.

132 *"Rabbi Joshua ben Levi"–Sanhedrin* 98a.

132 *Mishna–Sota* 9.15.

133 *Zohar–*Vol. II, 12b.

About JEWISH LIGHTS Publishing

People of all faiths and backgrounds yearn for books that attract, engage, educate and spiritually inspire.

Our principal goal is to stimulate thought and help all people learn about who the Jewish People are, where they come from, and what the future can be made to hold. While people of our diverse Jewish heritage are the primary audience, our books speak to people in the Christian world as well and will broaden their understanding of Judaism and the roots of their own faith.

We bring to you authors who are at the forefront of spiritual thought and experience. While each has something different to say, they all say it in a voice that you can hear.

Our books are designed to welcome you and then to engage, stimulate and inspire. We judge our success not only by whether or not our books are beautiful and commercially successful, but by whether or not they make a difference in your life.

We at Jewish Lights take great care to produce beautiful books that present meaningful spiritual content in a form that reflects the art of making high quality books. Therefore, we want to acknowledge those who contributed to the production of this book.

PRODUCTION
Bronwen Battaglia

EDITORIAL & PROOFREADING
Jennifer Goneau & Martha McKinney

COVER DESIGN
Glenn Suokko

COVER PRINTING
John P. Pow Company, South Boston, Massachusetts

PRINTING AND BINDING
Book Press, Brattleboro, Vermont

Spirituality—The Kushner Series

INVISIBLE LINES OF CONNECTION
Sacred Stories of the Ordinary
by *Lawrence Kushner*

Through his everyday encounters with family, friends, colleagues and strangers, Kushner takes us deeply into our lives, finding flashes of spiritual insight in the process. This is a book where literature meets spirituality, where the sacred meets the ordinary, and, above all, where people of all faiths, all backgrounds can meet one another and themselves.

•AWARD WINNER• "Does something both more and different than instruct—it inspirits. Wonderful stories, from the best storyteller I know."
— David Mamet

5 1/2" x 8 1/2", 160 pp. Quality Paperback, ISBN 1-879045-98-2 **$15.95** HC, -52-4 **$21.95**

HONEY FROM THE ROCK
An Easy Introduction to Jewish Mysticism
by *Lawrence Kushner*
"Quite simply the easiest introduction to Jewish mysticism you can read."

An introduction to the ten gates of Jewish mysticism and how it applies to daily life.

"Captures the flavor and spark of Jewish mysticism. . . . Read it and be rewarded." —*Elie Wiesel*

6" x 9", 168 pp. Quality Paperback, ISBN 1-879045-02-8 **$14.95**

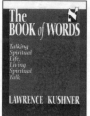

THE BOOK OF WORDS
Talking Spiritual Life, Living Spiritual Talk
by *Lawrence Kushner*

In the incomparable manner of his extraordinary *The Book of Letters*, Kushner now lifts up and shakes the dust off primary religious words we use to describe the spiritual dimension of life. For each word Kushner offers us a startling, moving and insightful explication, and pointed readings from classical Jewish sources that further illuminate the concept. He concludes with a short exercise that helps unite the spirit of the word with our actions in the world.

"This is a powerful and holy book."
—*M. Scott Peck, M.D., author of* The Road Less Traveled *and other books*

"What a delightful wholeness of intellectual vigor and meditative playfulness, and all in a tone of gentleness that speaks to this gentile."
—*Rt. Rev. Krister Stendahl, formerly Dean, Harvard Divinity School/Bishop of Stockholm*

6" x 9", 152 pp. 2-color text, Quality PB ISBN 1-58023-020-2 **$16.95**; HC, ISBN 1-879045-35-4 **$21.95**

THE BOOK OF LETTERS
A Mystical Hebrew Alphabet
by *Rabbi Lawrence Kushner*

In calligraphy by the author. Folktales about and exploration of the mystical meanings of the Hebrew Alphabet. Open the old prayerbook-like pages of *The Book of Letters* and you will enter a special world of sacred tradition and religious feeling. Rabbi Kushner draws from ancient Judaic sources, weaving talmudic commentary, Hasidic folktales, and kabbalistic mysteries around the letters.

"A book which is in love with Jewish letters."
— *Isaac Bashevis Singer* (ל׳ה)

•AWARD WINNER•

• **Popular Hardcover Edition** 6"x 9", 80 pp. HC, two colors, inspiring new Foreword. ISBN 1-879045-00-1 **$24.95**

• **Deluxe Gift Edition** 9"x 12", 80 pp. HC, four-color text, ornamentation, in a beautiful slipcase. ISBN 1-879045-01-X **$79.95**

• **Collector's Limited Edition** 9"x 12", 80 pp. HC, gold-embossed pages, hand-assembled slipcase. With silkscreened print. **Limited to 500 signed and numbered copies.** ISBN 1-879045-04-4 **$349.00**

To see a sample page at no obligation, call us

Spirituality

GOD WAS IN THIS PLACE & I, i DID NOT KNOW
Finding Self, Spirituality & Ultimate Meaning
by Lawrence Kushner

Who am I? Who is God? Kushner creates inspiring interpretations of Jacob's dream in Genesis, opening a window into Jewish spirituality for people of all faiths and backgrounds.

In this fascinating blend of scholarship, imagination, psychology and history, seven Jewish spiritual masters ask and answer fundamental questions of human experience.

"Rich and intriguing."
—*M. Scott Peck, M.D., author of* The Road Less Traveled *and other books*

6" x 9", 192 pp. Quality Paperback, ISBN 1-879045-33-8 **$16.95**

THE RIVER OF LIGHT
Spirituality, Judaism, Consciousness
by Lawrence Kushner

A "manual" for all spiritual travelers who would attempt a spiritual journey in our times. Taking us step by step, Kushner allows us to discover the meaning of our own quest: "to allow the river of light—the deepest currents of consciousness—to rise to the surface and animate our lives."

"Philosophy and mystical fantasy....Anybody—Jewish, Christian, or otherwise...will find this book an intriguing experience."
—*Kirkus Reviews*

6" x 9", 180 pp. Quality Paperback, ISBN 1-879045-03-6 **$14.95**

GODWRESTLING—ROUND 2
Ancient Wisdom, Future Paths
by Arthur Waskow

BEST RELIGION BOOK OF THE YEAR

This 20th-anniversary sequel to a seminal book of the Jewish renewal movement deals with spirituality in relation to personal growth, marriage, ecology, feminism, politics, and more. Including new chapters on recent issues and concerns, Waskow outlines original ways to merge "religious" life and "personal" life in our society today.

•AWARD WINNER•   "A delicious read and a soaring meditation."
—*Rabbi Zalman M. Schachter-Shalomi*

"Vivid as a novel, sharp, eccentric, loud....An important book for anyone who wants to bring Judaism alive."
—*Marge Piercy*

6" x 9", 352 pp. Quality Paperback, ISBN 1-879045-72-9 **$18.95** HC, ISBN-45-1 **$23.95**

BEING GOD'S PARTNER
How to Find the Hidden Link Between Spirituality and Your Work
by Jeffrey K. Salkin Introduction by *Norman Lear*

Will challenge people of every denomination to reconcile the cares of work and soul. A groundbreaking book about spirituality and the work world, from a Jewish perspective. Helps the reader find God in the ethical striving and search for meaning in the professions and in business and offers practical suggestions for balancing your professional life and spiritual self.

"This engaging meditation on the spirituality of work is grounded in Judaism but is relevant well beyond the boundaries of that tradition."
—*Booklist (American Library Association)*

6" x 9", 192 pp. Quality Paperback, ISBN 1-879045-65-6 **$16.95** HC, ISBN-37-0 **$19.95**

Spirituality

HOW TO BE A PERFECT STRANGER, In 2 Volumes
A Guide to Etiquette in Other People's Religious Ceremonies
Edited by *Stuart M. Matlins* & *Arthur J. Magida*

"A book that belongs in every living room, library and office!"

•AWARD WINNER•

Explains the rituals and celebrations of America's major religions/denominations, helping an interested guest to feel comfortable, participate to the fullest extent possible, and avoid violating anyone's religious principles. Answers practical questions from the perspective of *any* other faith.

VOL. 1: America's Largest Faiths

VOL. 1 COVERS: Assemblies of God • Baptist • Buddhist • Christian Science • Churches of Christ • Disciples of Christ • Episcopalian • Greek Orthodox • Hindu • Islam • Jehovah's Witnesses • Jewish • Lutheran • Methodist • Mormon • Presbyterian • Quaker • Roman Catholic • Seventh-day Adventist • United Church of Christ

6" x 9", 432 pp. Hardcover, ISBN 1-879045-39-7 **$24.95**

VOL. 2: Other Faiths in America

VOL. 2 COVERS: African American Methodist Churches • Baha'i • Christian and Missionary Alliance • Christian Congregation • Church of the Brethren • Church of the Nazarene • Evangelical Free Church of America • International Church of the Foursquare Gospel • International Pentecostal Holiness Church • Mennonite/Amish • Native American • Orthodox Churches • Pentecostal Church of God • Reformed Church of America • Sikh • Unitarian Universalist • Wesleyan

6" x 9", 416 pp. HC, ISBN 1-879045-63-X **$24.95**

GOD & THE BIG BANG
Discovering Harmony Between Science & Spirituality
by *Daniel C. Matt*

Mysticism and science: What do they have in common? How can one enlighten the other? By drawing on modern cosmology and ancient Kabbalah, Matt shows how science and religion can together enrich our spiritual awareness and help us recover a sense of wonder and find our place in the universe.

"This poetic new book...helps us to understand the human meaning of creation."
—*Joel Primack, leading cosmologist, Professor of Physics, University of California, Santa Cruz*

•AWARD WINNER•

6" x 9", 216 pp. Quality Paperback, ISBN 1-879045-89-3 **$16.95** HC, ISBN-48-6 **$21.95**

MINDING THE TEMPLE OF THE SOUL
Balancing Body, Mind, & Spirit through Traditional Jewish Prayer, Movement, & Meditation
by *Tamar Frankiel* and *Judy Greenfeld*

This new spiritual approach to physical health introduces readers to a spiritual tradition that affirms the body and enables them to reconceive their bodies in a more positive light. Relying on Kabbalistic teachings and other Jewish traditions, it shows us how to be more responsible for our own psychological and physical health. Focuses on the discipline of prayer, simple Tai Chi–like exercises and body positions, and guides the reader throughout, step-by-step, with diagrams, sketches and meditations.

7"x 10", 184 pp. Quality Paperback Original, illus., ISBN 1-879045-64-8 **$16.95**

Audiotape of the Blessings, Movements & Meditations (60-min. cassette) **$9.95**
Videotape of the Movements & Meditations (46-min. VHS) **$20.00**

Spirituality

MEDITATION FROM THE HEART OF JUDAISM
Today's Teachers Share Their Practices, Techniques, and Faith
Edited by *Avram Davis*

A "how-to" guide for both beginning and experienced meditators, it will help you start meditating or help you enhance your practice.

Twenty-two masters of meditation explain why and how they meditate. *A detailed compendium of the experts' "Best Practices"* offers practical advice and starting points.

"A treasury of meditative insights and techniques....Each page is a meditative experience that brings you closer to God."
— *Rabbi Shoni Labowitz, author of* Miraculous Living: A Guided Journey in Kabbalah through the Ten Gates of the Tree of Life

6" x 9", 256 pp. Hardcover, ISBN 1-879045-77-X **$21.95**

SELF, STRUGGLE & CHANGE
Family Conflict Stories in Genesis and Their Healing Insights for Our Lives
by *Norman J. Cohen*

How do I find greater wholeness in my life and in my family's life?

The people described by the biblical writers of Genesis were in situations and relationships very much like our own. We identify with them. Their stories still speak to us because they are about the same problems we deal with every day. Here a modern master of biblical interpretation brings us greater understanding of the ancient text and of ourselves in this intriguing re-telling of conflict between husband and wife, father and son, brothers, and sisters.

"Delightfully written...rare erudition, sensitivity and insight."   — *Elie Wiesel*
6" x 9", 224 pp. Quality Paperback, ISBN 1-879045-66-4 **$16.95**; HC, ISBN-19-2 **$21.95**

ECOLOGY & THE JEWISH SPIRIT
Where Nature & the Sacred Meet
Edited and with Introductions by *Ellen Bernstein*

What is nature's place in our spiritual lives?

A focus on nature is part of the fabric of Jewish thought. Here, experts bring us a richer understanding of the long-neglected themes of nature that are woven through the biblical creation story, ancient texts, traditional law, the holiday cycles, prayer, *mitzvot* (good deeds), and community.

For people of all faiths, all backgrounds, this book helps us to make nature a sacred, spiritual part of our own lives.

"A great resource for anyone seeking to explore the connection between their faith and caring for God's good creation, our environment."
— *Paul Gorman, Executive Director, National Religious Partnership for the Environment*
6" x 9", 288 pp. HC, ISBN 1-879045-88-5 **$23.95**

ISRAEL—A SPIRITUAL TRAVEL GUIDE
A Companion for the Modern Jewish Pilgrim
by *Rabbi Lawrence A. Hoffman*

Be spiritually prepared for your journey to Israel.

A Jewish spiritual travel guide to Israel, helping today's pilgrim tap into the deep spiritual meaning of the ancient—and modern—sites of the Holy Land. Combines in quick reference format ancient blessings, medieval prayers, biblical and historical references, and modern poetry. The only guidebook that helps readers to prepare spiritually for the occasion. More than a guide book: It is a spiritual map.

"To add spiritual dimension to your journey, pack this extraordinary new guidebook to Israel. I'll be bringing it on my next visit."
— *Gabe Levenson, travel columnist for* The New York Jewish Week

4 3/4" x 10 1/8", 256 pp. Quality Paperback Original, ISBN 1-879045-56-7 **$18.95**

Spirituality

MY PEOPLE'S PRAYER BOOK
Traditional Prayers, Modern Commentaries
Vol. 1—The *Sh'ma* and Its Blessings
Vol. 2—The *Amidah*
Edited by *Rabbi Lawrence A. Hoffman*

Provides a diverse and exciting commentary to the traditional liturgy, written by 10 of today's most respected scholars and teachers from all perspectives of the Jewish world.

With 7 volumes published semiannually until completion of the series, this stunning work enables all of us to be involved in a personal dialogue with God, history and tradition through the heritage of the prayer book.

"This book engages the mind and heart....It challenges one's assumptions at whatever level of understanding one brings to the text." —*Jewish Herald-Voice*

Vol. 1: 7" x 10", 168 pp. HC, ISBN 1-879045-79-6 **$19.95**
Vol. 2: 7" x 10", 200 pp. (est.) HC, ISBN 1-879045-80-X **$21.95**

FINDING JOY
A Practical Spiritual Guide to Happiness
by *Dannel I. Schwartz* with *Mark Hass*

Searching for happiness in our modern world of stress and struggle is common; *finding* it is more unusual. This guide explores and explains how to find joy through a time-honored, creative—and surprisingly practical—approach based on the teachings of Jewish mysticism and Kabbalah.

"Lovely, simple introduction to Kabbalah....a singular contribution...."
—*American Library Association's* Booklist

•AWARD WINNER•

6" x 9", 192 pp. Quality PB, ISBN 1-58023-009-1 **$14.95** HC, ISBN 1-879045-53-2 **$19.95**

THE DEATH OF DEATH
Resurrection and Immortality in Jewish Thought
by *Neil Gillman*

Noted theologian Neil Gillman explores the original and compelling argument that Judaism, a religion often thought to pay little attention to the afterlife, not only offers us rich ideas on the subject—but delivers a deathblow to death itself. By exploring Jewish thought about death and the afterlife, this fascinating work presents us with challenging new ideas about our lives.

"Enables us to recover our tradition's understanding of the afterlife and breaks through the silence of modern Jewish thought on immortality.... A work of major •AWARD WINNER• significance."
—*Rabbi Sheldon Zimmerman, President, Hebrew Union College–Jewish Institute of Religion*

6" x 9", 336 pp., HC, ISBN 1-879045-61-3 **$23.95**

THE EMPTY CHAIR: FINDING HOPE & JOY
Timeless Wisdom from a Hasidic Master,
Rebbe Nachman of Breslov
Adapted by Moshe Mykoff and the Breslov Research Institute

A "little treasure" of aphorisms and advice for living joyously and spiritually today, written 200 years ago, but startlingly fresh in meaning and use. Challenges and helps us to move from stress and sadness to hope and joy.

Teacher, guide and spiritual master—Rebbe Nachman provides vital words of inspiration and wisdom for life today for people of any faith, or of no faith.

•AWARD WINNER•

"For anyone of any faith, this is a book of healing and wholeness, of being alive!"
— *Bookviews*

4" x 6", 128 pp., 2-color text, Deluxe Paperback, ISBN 1-879045-67-2 **$9.95**

Art of Jewish Living Series for Holiday Observance

THE SHABBAT SEDER
by *Dr. Ron Wolfson*

A concise step-by-step guide designed to teach people the meaning and importance of this weekly celebration, as well as its practices.

Each chapter corresponds to one of ten steps which together comprise the Shabbat dinner ritual, and looks at the *concepts, objects,* and *meanings* behind the specific activity or ritual act. The blessings that accompany the meal are written in both Hebrew and English, and accompanied by English transliteration. Also included are craft projects, recipes, discussion ideas and other creative suggestions for enriching the Shabbat experience.

"A how-to book in the best sense...."
—*Dr. David Lieber, President, University of Judaism, Los Angeles*

7" x 9", 272 pp. Quality Paperback, ISBN 1-879045-90-7 **$16.95**

Also available are these helpful companions to *The Shabbat Seder*:
- •Booklet of the Blessings and Songs   ISBN 1-879045-91-5 $5.00
- •Audiocassette of the Blessings   DNO3 $6.00
- •Teacher's Guide   ISBN 1-879045-92-3 $4.95

HANUKKAH
by *Dr. Ron Wolfson*
Edited by *Joel Lurie Grishaver*

Designed to help celebrate and enrich the holiday season, *Hanukkah* discusses the holiday's origins, explores the reasons for the Hanukkah candles and customs, and provides everything from recipes to family activities.

There are songs, recipes, useful information on the arts and crafts of Hanukkah, the calendar and its relationship to Christmas time, and games played at Hanukkah. Putting the holiday in a larger, timely context, "December Dilemmas" deals with ways in which a Jewish family can cope with Christmas.

"Helpful for the family that strives to induct its members into the spirituality and joys of Jewishness and Judaism...a significant text in the neglected art of Jewish family education."
—*Rabbi Harold M. Schulweis, Cong. Valley Beth Shalom, Encino, CA*

7" x 9", 192 pp. Quality Paperback, ISBN 1-879045-97-4 **$16.95**

THE PASSOVER SEDER
by *Dr. Ron Wolfson*

Explains the concepts behind Passover ritual and ceremony in clear, easy-to-understand language, and offers step-by-step procedures for Passover observance and preparing the home for the holiday.

Easy-to-Follow Format: Using an innovative photo-documentary technique, real families describe in vivid images their own experiences with the Passover holiday. **Easy-to-Read Hebrew Texts:** The Haggadah texts in Hebrew, English, and transliteration are presented in a three-column format designed to help celebrants learn the meaning of the prayers and how to read them. **An Abundance of Useful Information:** A detailed description of how to perform the rituals is included, along with practical questions and answers, and imaginative ideas for Seder celebration.

"A creative 'how-to' for making the Seder a more meaningful experience."
—*Michael Strassfeld, co-author of* The Jewish Catalog

7" x 9", 336 pp. Quality Paperback, ISBN 1-879045-93-1 **$16.95**

Also available are these helpful companions to *The Passover Seder*:
- •Passover Workbook   ISBN 1-879045-94-X $6.95
- •Audiocassette of the Blessings   DNO4 $6.00
- •Teacher's Guide   ISBN 1-879045-95-8 $4.95

Life Cycle

GRIEF IN OUR SEASONS
A Mourner's Kaddish Companion
by *Rabbi Kerry M. Olitzky*

Strength from the Jewish tradition for the first year of mourning.

Provides a wise and inspiring selection of sacred Jewish writings and a simple, powerful ancient ritual for mourners to read each day, to help hold the memory of their loved ones in their hearts. It offers a comforting, step-by-step daily link to saying *Kaddish*.

"A hopeful, compassionate guide along the journey from grief to rebirth from mourning to a new morning."
　　　　　—*Rabbi Levi Meier, Ph.D., Chaplain, Cedars–Sinai Medical Center, Los Angeles*

4 1/2" x 6 1/2", 448 pp., Quality Paperback Original, ISBN 1-879045-55-9 **$15.95**

MOURNING & MITZVAH　　• WITH OVER 60 GUIDED EXERCISES •
A Guided Journal for Walking the Mourner's Path Through Grief to Healing
by *Anne Brener, L.C.S.W.*; Foreword by *Rabbi Jack Riemer*; Introduction by *Rabbi William Cutter*

"Fully engaging in mourning means you will be a different person than before you began." **For those who mourn a death, for those who would help them,** for those who face a loss of any kind, Brener teaches us the power and strength available to us in the fully experienced mourning process. Guided writing exercises help stimulate the processes of both conscious and unconscious healing.

"A stunning book! It offers an exploration in depth of the place where psychology and religious ritual intersect, and the name of that place is Truth."
　　　　　—*Rabbi Harold Kushner, author of* When Bad Things Happen to Good People

7 1/2" x 9", 288 pp. Quality Paperback Original, ISBN 1-879045-23-0 **$19.95**

A TIME TO MOURN, A TIME TO COMFORT
A Guide to Jewish Bereavement and Comfort
by *Dr. Ron Wolfson*

A guide to meeting the needs of those who mourn and those who seek to provide comfort in times of sadness. While this book is written from a layperson's point of view, it also includes the specifics for funeral preparations and practical guidance for preparing the home and family to sit *shiva*.

"A sensitive and perceptive guide to Jewish tradition. Both those who mourn and those who comfort will find it a map to accompany them through the whirlwind."
　　　　　—*Deborah E. Lipstadt, Emory University*
7" x 9", 320 pp. Quality Paperback, ISBN 1-879045-96-6 **$16.95**

WHEN A GRANDPARENT DIES
A Kid's Own Remembering Workbook for Dealing with Shiva and the Year Beyond
by *Nechama Liss-Levinson, Ph.D.*

Drawing insights from both psychology and Jewish tradition, this workbook helps children participate in the process of mourning, offering guided exercises, rituals, and places to write, draw, list, create and express their feelings.

"Will bring support, guidance, and understanding for countless children, teachers, and health professionals."
　　　　　—*Rabbi Earl A. Grollman, D.D., author of* Talking about Death

8" x 10", 48 pp. HC, illus., 2-color text, ISBN 1-879045-44-3 **$15.95**

Life Cycle

A HEART OF WISDOM
Making the Jewish Journey from Midlife Through the Elder Years
Edited by *Susan Berrin*

We are all growing older. *A Heart of Wisdom* shows us how to understand our own process of aging—and the aging of those we care about—from a Jewish perspective, from midlife through the elder years.

How does Jewish tradition influence our own aging? How does living, thinking and worshipping as a Jew affect us as we age? How can Jewish tradition help us retain our dignity as we age? Offers insights and enlightenment from Jewish tradition.

"A thoughtfully orchestrated collection of pieces that deal candidly and compassionately with a period of growing concern to us all: midlife through old age."
—*Chaim Potok*

6" x 9", 384 pp. HC, ISBN 1 879045-73-7 **$24.95**

LIFECYCLES
V. 1: Jewish Women on Life Passages & Personal Milestones
Edited and with Introductions by *Rabbi Debra Orenstein*
V. 2: Jewish Women on Biblical Themes in Contemporary Life
Edited and with Introductions by
Rabbi Debra Orenstein and *Rabbi Jane Rachel Litman*

This unique multivolume collaboration brings together over one hundred women writers, rabbis, and scholars to create the first comprehensive work on Jewish life cycle that fully includes women's perspectives.

"Nothing is missing from this marvelous collection. You will turn to it for rituals and inspiration, prayer and poetry, comfort and community. *Lifecycles* is a gift to the Jewish woman in America."
—*Letty Cottin Pogrebin, author of* Deborah, Golda, and Me: Being Female and Jewish in America

•AWARD WINNER•

V. 1: 6" x 9", 480 pp. HC, ISBN 1-879045-14-1, **$24.95**; V. 2: 6" x 9", 464 pp. HC, ISBN 1-879045-15-X, **$24.95**

LIFE CYCLE— The Art of Jewish Living Series for Holiday Observance
by Dr. Ron Wolfson

Hanukkah—7" x 9", 192 pp. Quality Paperback, ISBN 1-879045-97-4 **$16.95**

The Shabbat Seder—7" x 9", 272 pp. Quality Paperback, ISBN 1-879045-90-7 **$16.95**; Booklet of Blessings **$5.00**; Audiocassette of Blessings **$6.00**; Teacher's Guide **$4.95**

The Passover Seder—7" x 9", 336 pp. Quality Paperback, ISBN 1-879045 93 1 **$16.95**; Passover Workbook, **$6.95**; Audiocassette of Blessings, **$6.00**; Teacher's Guide, **$4.95**

LIFE CYCLE...Other Books

Bar/Bat Mitzvah Basics: A Practical Family Guide to Coming of Age Together
Ed. by Cantor Helen Leneman 6" x 9", 240 pp. Quality Paperback, ISBN 1-879045-54-0 **$16.95**

Embracing the Covenant: Converts to Judaism Talk About Why & How
Ed. and with Intros. by Rabbi Allan L. Berkowitz and Patti Moskovitz
6" x 9", 192 pp. Quality Paperback, ISBN 1-879045-50-8 **$15.95**

The New Jewish Baby Book: Names, Ceremonies, Customs—A Guide for Today's Families by Anita Diamant 6" x 9", 336 pp. Quality Paperback, ISBN 1-879045-28-1 **$16.95**

Putting God on the Guest List, 2nd Ed.: How to Reclaim the Spiritual Meaning of Your Child's Bar or Bat Mitzvah by Rabbi Jeffrey K. Salkin 6" x 9", 224 pp. Quality Paperback, ISBN 1-897045-59-1 **$16.95**; HC, ISBN 1-879045-58-3 **$24.95**

So That Your Values Live On: Ethical Wills & How to Prepare Them
Ed. by Rabbi Jack Riemer & Professor Nathaniel Stampfer
6" x 9", 272 pp. Quality Paperback, ISBN 1-879045-34-6 **$17.95**

Theology/Philosophy

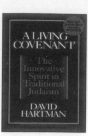

•AWARD WINNER•

A LIVING COVENANT
The Innovative Spirit in Traditional Judaism
by *David Hartman*

*WINNER,
National Jewish
Book Award*

The Judaic tradition is often seen as being more concerned with uncritical obedience to law than with individual freedom and responsibility. Hartman challenges this approach by revealing a Judaism grounded in a covenant—a relational framework—informed by the metaphor of marital love rather than that of parent-child dependency.

"Jews and non-Jews, liberals and traditionalists will see classic Judaism anew in these pages."
　　　　　　—Dr. Eugene B. Borowitz, *Hebrew Union College–Jewish Institute of Religion*
6" x 9", 368 pp. Quality Paperback, ISBN 1-58023-011-3 **$18.95**

THE SPIRIT OF RENEWAL
Finding Faith after the Holocaust
by *Edward Feld*

Trying to understand the Holocaust and addressing the question of faith after the Holocaust, Rabbi Feld explores three key cycles of destruction and recovery in Jewish history, each of which radically reshaped Jewish understanding of God, people, and the world.

"A profound meditation on Jewish history [and the Holocaust]....Christians, as well as many others, need to share in this story."
　　　　　　—The Rt. Rev. Frederick H. Borsch, Ph.D., *Episcopal Bishop of L.A.*

•AWARD WINNER•

6" x 9", 224 pp. Quality Paperback, ISBN 1-879045-40-0 **$16.95**

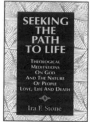

SEEKING THE PATH TO LIFE
Theological Meditations On God
and the Nature of People, Love, Life and Death
by *Rabbi Ira F. Stone*

For people who never thought they would read a book of theology—let alone understand it, enjoy it, savor it and have it affect the way they think about their lives. In 45 intense meditations, each a page or two in length, Stone takes us on explorations of the most basic human struggles: Life and death, love and anger, peace and war, covenant and exile.

•AWARD WINNER•　　"A bold book....The reader of any faith will be inspired...."
　　　　　　— The Rev. Carla V. Berkedal, *Episcopal Priest*
6" x 9", 132 pp. Quality Paperback, ISBN 1-879045-47-8 **$14.95** HC, ISBN-17-6 **$19.95**

CLASSICS BY ABRAHAM JOSHUA HESCHEL

The Earth Is the Lord's: The Inner World of the Jew in Eastern Europe
5 1/2" x 8", 112 pp, Quality Paperback, ISBN 1-879045-42-7 **$13.95**

Israel: An Echo of Eternity with new Introduction by Susannah Heschel
5 1/2" x 8", 272 pp, Quality Paperback, ISBN 1-879045-70-2 **$18.95**

A Passion for Truth: Despair and Hope in Hasidism
5 1/2" x 8", 352 pp, Quality Paperback, ISBN 1-879045-41-9 **$18.95**

THEOLOGY & PHILOSOPHY...Other books—Classic Reprints

Aspects of Rabbinic Theology by Solomon Schechter, with a new Introduction
by Neil Gillman 6" x 9", 440 pp, Quality Paperback, ISBN 1-879045-24-9 **$18.95**

*The Last Trial: On the Legends and Lore of the Command to Abraham to Offer
Isaac as a Sacrifice* by Shalom Spiegel, with a new Introduction by Judah Goldin
6" x 9", 208 pp, Quality Paperback, ISBN 1-879045-29-X **$17.95**

Judaism and Modern Man: An Interpretation of Jewish Religion by Will Herberg; new
Introduction by Neil Gillman 5.5" x 8.5", 336 pp, Quality Paperback, ISBN 1-879045-87-7 **$18.95**

Tormented Master: The Life and Spiritual Quest of Rabbi Nahman of Bratslav
by Arthur Green 6" x 9", 408 pp, Quality Paperback, ISBN 1-879045-11-7 **$18.95**

Your Word Is Fire Ed. and trans. with a new Introduction by Arthur Green and
Barry W. Holtz 6" x 9", 152 pp, Quality Paperback, ISBN 1-879045-25-7 **$14.95**

Healing/Recovery/Wellness

Experts Praise *Twelve Jewish Steps to Recovery*

"Recommended reading for people of all denominations."
—*Rabbi Abraham J. Twerski, M.D.*

TWELVE JEWISH STEPS TO RECOVERY
A Personal Guide to Turning from Alcoholism & Other Addictions...Drugs, Food, Gambling, Sex...
by *Rabbi Kerry M. Olitzky & Stuart A. Copans, M.D.*
Preface by *Abraham J. Twerski, M.D.*; Intro. by *Rabbi Sheldon Zimmerman*; "Getting Help" by *JACS Foundation*

A Jewish perspective on the Twelve Steps of addiction recovery programs with consolation, inspiration and motivation for recovery. It draws from traditional sources and quotes from what recovering Jewish people say about their experiences with addictions of all kinds. Inspiring illustrations of the twelve gates of the Old City of Jerusalem introduce each step.

6" x 9", 136 pp. Quality Paperback, ISBN 1-879045-09-5 **$13.95**

Recovery from Codependence: A Jewish Twelve Steps Guide to Healing Your Soul
by Rabbi Kerry M. Olitzky

6" x 9", 160 pp. Quality Paperback Original, ISBN 1-879045-32-X **$13.95** HC, ISBN-27-3 **$21.95**

Renewed Each Day: Daily Twelve Step Recovery Meditations Based on the Bible
by Rabbi Kerry M. Olitzky & Aaron Z.

6" x 9", Quality Paperback Original, **V. I**, 224 pp. **$14.95** **V. II**, 280 pp. **$16.95**
Two-Volume Set ISBN 1-879045-21-4 **$27.90**

One Hundred Blessings Every Day: Daily Twelve Step Recovery Affirmations, Exercises for Personal Growth & Renewal Reflecting Seasons of the Jewish Year
by Rabbi Kerry M. Olitzky

4 1/2" x 6 1/2", 432 pp. Quality Paperback Original, ISBN 1-879045-30-3 **$14.95**

HEALING OF SOUL, HEALING OF BODY
Spiritual Leaders Unfold the Strength and Solace in Psalms
Edited by *Rabbi Simkha Y. Weintraub, CSW, for The Jewish Healing Center*

A source of solace for those who are facing illness, as well as those who care for them. The ten Psalms which form the core of this healing resource were originally selected 200 years ago by Rabbi Nachman of Breslov as a "complete remedy." Today, for anyone coping with illness, they continue to provide a wellspring of strength. Each Psalm is newly translated, making it clear and accessible, and each one is introduced by an eminent rabbi, men and women reflecting different movements and backgrounds. To all who are living with the pain and uncertainty of illness, this spiritual resource offers an anchor of spiritual comfort.

"Will bring comfort to anyone fortunate enough to read it. This gentle book is a luminous gem of wisdom."
—*Larry Dossey, M.D., author of* Healing Words: The Power of Prayer & the Practice of Medicine

6" x 9", 128 pp. Quality Paperback Original, illus., 2-color text, ISBN 1-879045-31-1 **$14.95**

Children's Spirituality

A PRAYER FOR THE EARTH
The Story of Naamah, Noah's Wife

For ages 4 and up

by *Sandy Eisenberg Sasso*
Full-color illustrations by *Bethanne Andersen*

NONDENOMINATIONAL, NONSECTARIAN

This new story, based on an ancient text, opens readers' religious imaginations to new ideas about the well-known story of the Flood. When God tells Noah to bring the animals of the world onto the ark, God *also* calls on Naamah, Noah's wife, to save each plant on Earth.

> "A lovely tale....Children of all ages should be drawn to this parable for our times."
>
> —*Tomie dePaola, artist/author of books for children*

•AWARD WINNER•

9" x 12", 32 pp. HC, Full-color illus., ISBN 1-879045-60-5 **$16.95**

THE 11TH COMMANDMENT
Wisdom from Our Children
For all ages

by The Children of America

MULTICULTURAL, NONDENOMINATIONAL, NONSECTARIAN

"If there were an Eleventh Commandment, what would it be?"

Children of many religious denominations across America answer this question—in their own drawings and words—in *The 11th Commandment.*

> "Wonderful....This unusual book provides both food for thought and insight into the hopes and fears of today's young."
> —*American Library Association's* Booklist

8" x 10", 48 pp. HC, Full-color illus., ISBN 1-879045-46-X **$16.95**

SHARING BLESSINGS
Children's Stories for Exploring the Spirit of the Jewish Holidays

For ages 6 and up

by *Rahel Musleah* and *Rabbi Michael Klayman*
Full-color illustrations by *Mary O'Keefe Young*

What is the spiritual message of each of the Jewish holidays?
How do we teach it to our children?

Many books tell children about the historical significance and customs of the holidays. Now, through engaging, creative stories about one family's spiritual preparation, *Sharing Blessings* explores ways to get into the *spirit* of 13 different holidays.

> "A beguiling introduction to important Jewish values by way of the holidays."
> —*Rabbi Harold Kushner, author of* When Bad Things Happen to Good People *and* How Good Do We Have to Be?

7" x 10", 64 pp. HC, Full-color illus., ISBN 1-879045-71-0 **$18.95**

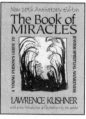

THE BOOK OF MIRACLES
For ages 9–13
A Young Person's Guide to Jewish Spiritual Awareness

by *Lawrence Kushner*

With a Special 10th Anniversary Introduction and all new illustrations by the author.

From the miracle at the Red Sea to the miracle of waking up this morning, this intriguing book introduces kids to a way of everyday spiritual thinking to last a lifetime. Kushner, whose award-winning books have brought spirituality to life for countless adults, now shows young people how to use Judaism as a foundation on which to build their lives.

6" x 9", 96 pp. HC, 2-color illus., ISBN 1-879045-78-8 **$16.95**

Children's Spirituality

For ages 8 and up

BUT GOD REMEMBERED
Stories of Women from Creation to the Promised Land
by *Sandy Eisenberg Sasso*
Full-color illustrations by *Bethanne Andersen*

NONDENOMINATIONAL, NONSECTARIAN

A fascinating collection of four different stories of women only briefly mentioned in biblical tradition and religious texts, but never before explored. Award-winning author Sasso brings to life the intriguing stories of Lilith, Serach, Bityah, and the Daughters of Z, courageous and strong women from ancient tradition. All teach important values through their faith and actions.

•AWARD WINNER•

"Exquisite....a book of beauty, strength and spirituality."
—*Association of Bible Teachers*

9" x 12", 32 pp. HC, Full-color illus., ISBN 1-879045-43-5 **$16.95**

IN GOD'S NAME

For ages 4 and up

by *Sandy Eisenberg Sasso*
Full-color illustrations by *Phoebe Stone*

MULTICULTURAL, NONDENOMINATIONAL, NONSECTARIAN

Like an ancient myth in its poetic text and vibrant illustrations, this modern fable about the search for God's name celebrates the diversity and, at the same time, the unity of all the people of the world. Each seeker claims he or she alone knows the answer. Finally, they come together and learn what God's name really is, sharing the ultimate harmony of belief in one God by people of all faiths, all backgrounds.

•AWARD WINNER•

"I got goose bumps when I read *In God's Name*, its language and illustrations are that moving. This is a book children will love and the whole family will cherish for its beauty and power."
—*Francine Klagsbrun, author of* Mixed Feelings: Love, Hate, Rivalry, and Reconciliation among Brothers and Sisters

"What a lovely, healing book!"
—*Madeleine L'Engle*

> Selected by
> Parent Council, Ltd.™

9" x 12", 32 pp. HC, Full color illus., ISBN 1-879045-26-5 **$16.95**

For ages 4 and up

GOD'S PAINTBRUSH
by *Sandy Eisenberg Sasso*
Full-color illustrations by *Annette Compton*

MULTICULTURAL, NONDENOMINATIONAL, NONSECTARIAN

Invites children of all faiths and backgrounds to encounter God openly in their own lives. Wonderfully interactive, provides questions adult and child can explore together at the end of each episode.

"An excellent way to honor the imaginative breadth and depth of the spiritual life of the young."
—*Dr. Robert Coles, Harvard University*

•AWARD WINNER•

11" x 8 1/2", 32 pp. HC, Full-color illus., ISBN 1-879045-22-2 **$16.95**

Also Available!
Teacher's Guide: A Guide for Jewish & Christian Educators and Parents
8 1/2" x 11", 32 pp. PB, ISBN 1-879045-57-5 **$6.95**

New from Jewish Lights

"WHO IS A JEW?"
Conversations, Not Conclusions
by *Meryl Hyman*

Who is "Jewish enough" to be considered a Jew? And by whom?

Meryl Hyman courageously takes on this timely and controversial question to give readers the perspective necessary to draw their own conclusions. With the skill of a seasoned journalist, she weaves her own life experiences into this complex and controversial story. Profound personal questions of identity are explored in conversations with Jew and non-Jew in the U.S., Israel and England. *"Who Is a Jew?"* is a book for those who seek to understand the issue, and for those who think they already do.

6" x 9", 272 pp. HC, ISBN 1-879045-76-1 **$23.95**

THE JEWISH GARDENING COOKBOOK
Growing Plants and Cooking for Holidays & Festivals
by *Michael Brown*

Through gardening and cooking for holiday and festival use, we can recover and discover many exciting aspects of Judaism to nourish both the mind and the spirit. Whether you garden in an herb garden, on a city apartment windowsill or patio, or on an acre, with the fruits and vegetables of your own gardening labors, the traditional repasts of Jewish holidays and celebrations can be understood in many new ways!

Gives easy-to-follow instructions for raising foods that have been harvested since ancient times. Provides carefully selected, tasty and easy-to-prepare recipes using these traditional foodstuffs for holidays, festivals, and life cycle events. Clearly illustrated with more than 30 fine botanical illustrations. For beginner and professional alike.

6" x 9", 224 pp. HC, ISBN 1-58023-004-0 **$21.95**

WANDERING STARS
An Anthology of Jewish Fantasy & Science Fiction
Edited by *Jack Dann; with an Introduction by Isaac Asimov*

Jewish science fiction and fantasy? *Yes!*

Here is the distinguished list of contributors to *Wandering Stars*, originally published in 1974 and the only book of its kind, anywhere: Bernard Malamud, Isaac Bashevis Singer, Isaac Asimov, Robert Silverberg, Harlan Ellison, Pamela Sargent, Avram Davidson, Geo. Alec Effinger, Horace L. Gold, Robert Sheckley, William Tenn and Carol Carr. Pure enjoyment. We laughed out loud reading it. A 25th Anniversary Classic Reprint.

"It is delightful and deep, hilarious and sad." —*James Morrow, author*, Towing Jehovah

6" x 9", 272 pp. Quality Paperback, ISBN 1-58023-005-9 **$16.95**

THE ENNEAGRAM AND KABBALAH
Reading Your Soul
by *Rabbi Howard A. Addison*

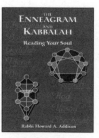

What do the Enneagram and *Kabbalah* have in common? Together, can they provide a powerful tool for self-knowledge, critique, and transformation?

How can we distinguish between acquired personality traits and the essential self hidden underneath?

6" x 9", 176 pp. Quality Paperback Original, ISBN 1-58023-001-6 **$15.95**

AVAILABLE FROM BETTER BOOKSTORES.
TRY YOUR BOOKSTORE FIRST.

Order Information

# of Copies	Book Title / ISBN (Last 3 digits)	$ Amount
_____	_____	_____
_____	_____	_____
_____	_____	_____
_____	_____	_____
_____	_____	_____
_____	_____	_____
_____	_____	_____
_____	_____	_____
_____	_____	_____
_____	_____	_____
_____	_____	_____
_____	_____	_____
_____	_____	_____

For shipping/handling, add $3.50 for the first book, $2.00 each
add'l book (to a max of $15.00)   **$ S/H** _____

TOTAL _____

Check enclosed for $_____ *payable to:* JEWISH LIGHTS Publishing

Charge my credit card: ❏ MasterCard   ❏ Visa

Credit Card #_____Expires _____

Signature _____Phone (_____)_____

Your Name _____

Street_____

City / State / Zip _____

Ship To:

Name _____

Street_____

City / State / Zip _____

Phone, fax or mail to: **JEWISH LIGHTS Publishing**
Sunset Farm Offices, Route 4 • P.O. Box 237 • Woodstock, Vermont 05091
Tel (802) 457-4000   Fax (802) 457-4004   www.jewishlights.com
Credit card orders (800) 962-4544 (9AM–5PM ET Monday–Friday)
Generous discounts on quantity orders. SATISFACTION GUARANTEED. Prices subject to change.

New from Jewish Lights

PARENTING AS A SPIRITUAL JOURNEY
Deepening Ordinary & Extraordinary Events into Sacred Occasions
by *Rabbi Nancy Fuchs-Kreimer*

A perfect gift for the new parent, and a helpful guidebook for those seeking to re-envision family life.

Draws on experiences of the author and over 100 parents of many faiths, revealing the transformative spiritual adventure that parents can experience while bringing up their children. Rituals, prayers, and passages from sacred Jewish texts—as well as from other religious traditions—are woven throughout the book.

"This is really relevant spirituality. I love her book."
—*Sylvia Boorstein, author of* It's Easier Than You Think *and mother of four*

6" x 9", 224 pp. Quality Paperback, ISBN 1-58023-016-4 **$16.95**

STEPPING STONES TO JEWISH SPIRITUAL LIVING
Walking the Path Morning, Noon, and Night
by *Rabbi James L. Mirel & Karen Bonnell Werth*

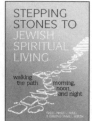

How can we bring the sacred into our busy lives?

Transforms our daily routine into sacred acts of mindfulness. Chapters are arranged according to the cycle of each day—and the cycle of our lives—providing spiritual activities, creative new rituals, meditations, acts of *kavannah* (spiritual intention) and prayers for any lifestyle, to help us embrace God's creation every moment.

"A wonderful, practical, and inspiring guidebook to gently bring the riches of Jewish practice into our busy, everyday lives. Highly recommended."
—*Rabbi David Cooper, author of* God Is a Verb

6" x 9", 240 pp. HC, ISBN 1-58023-003-2 **$21.95**

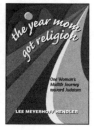

THE YEAR MOM GOT RELIGION
One Woman's Midlife Journey toward Judaism
by *Lee Meyerhoff Hendler*

A frank, thoughtful, and humorous "spiritual autobiography" that will speak to anyone in search of deeper meaning in their religious life.

The author shares with the reader the hard lessons and realizations she confronted as a result of her awakening to Judaism, including how her transformation deeply affected her lifestyle and relationships. Hendler's journey is a powerful reminder that anyone, at any moment, can deeply embrace faith—and face the challenges that occur along the way.

6" x 9", 200 pp. (est) HC, ISBN 1-58023-000-8 **$19.95**

MOSES, THE PRINCE OF EGYPT
His Life, Legend & Message for Our Lives
by *Rabbi Levi Meier, Ph.D.*

How can the struggles of a great biblical figure teach us to cope with our own lives today?

A fascinating portrait of the struggles, failures, and triumphs of Moses, a central figure in Jewish, Christian, and Islamic tradition. Drawing upon stories from *Exodus, midrash* (finding contemporary meaning from ancient Jewish texts), the teachings of Jewish mystics, modern texts, and psychotherapy, Meier offers new ways to create our own path to self-knowledge and self-fulfillment—and face life's difficulties head-on.

6" x 9", 225 pp. (est) HC, ISBN 1-58023-013-X **$23.95**